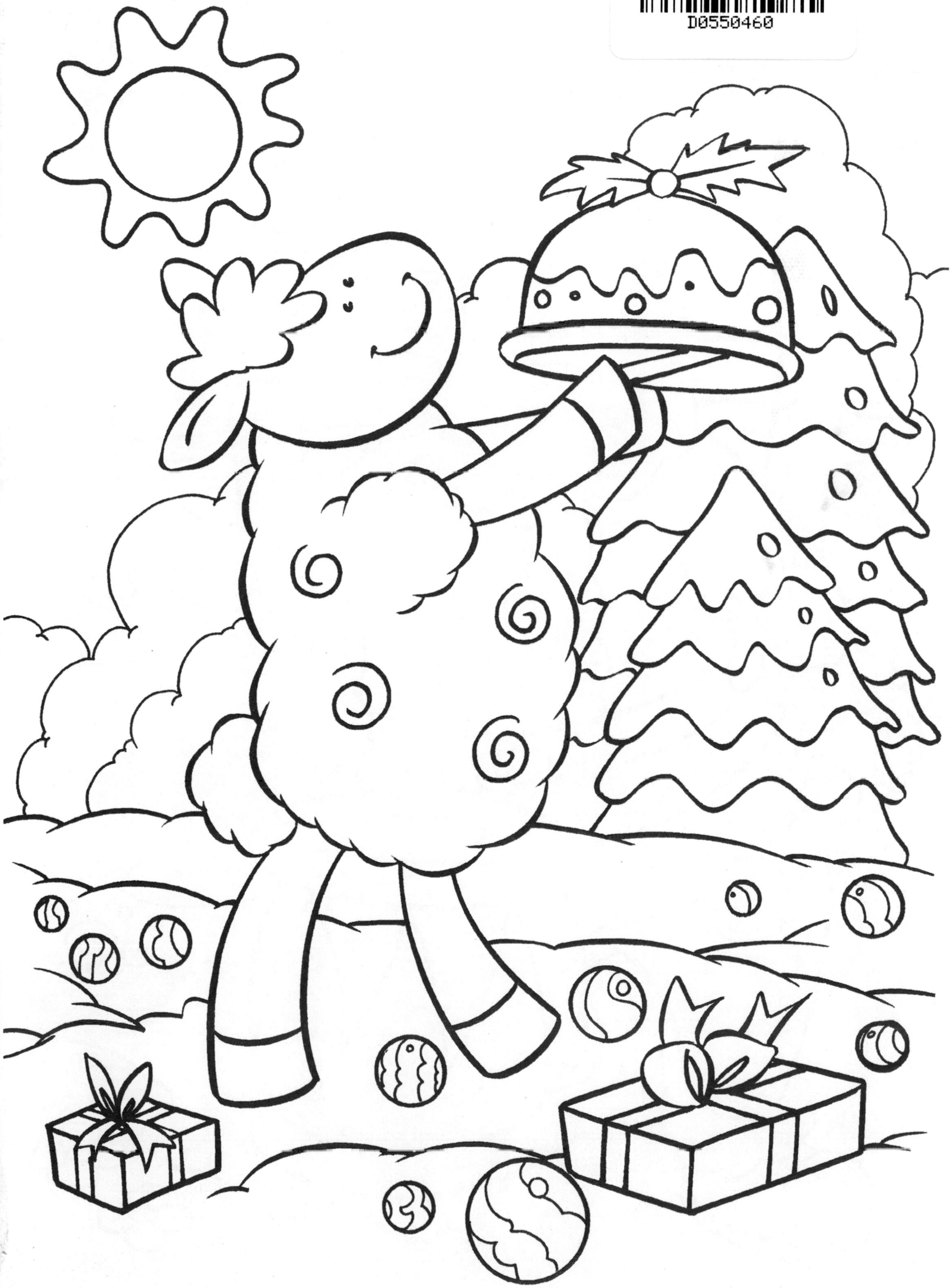

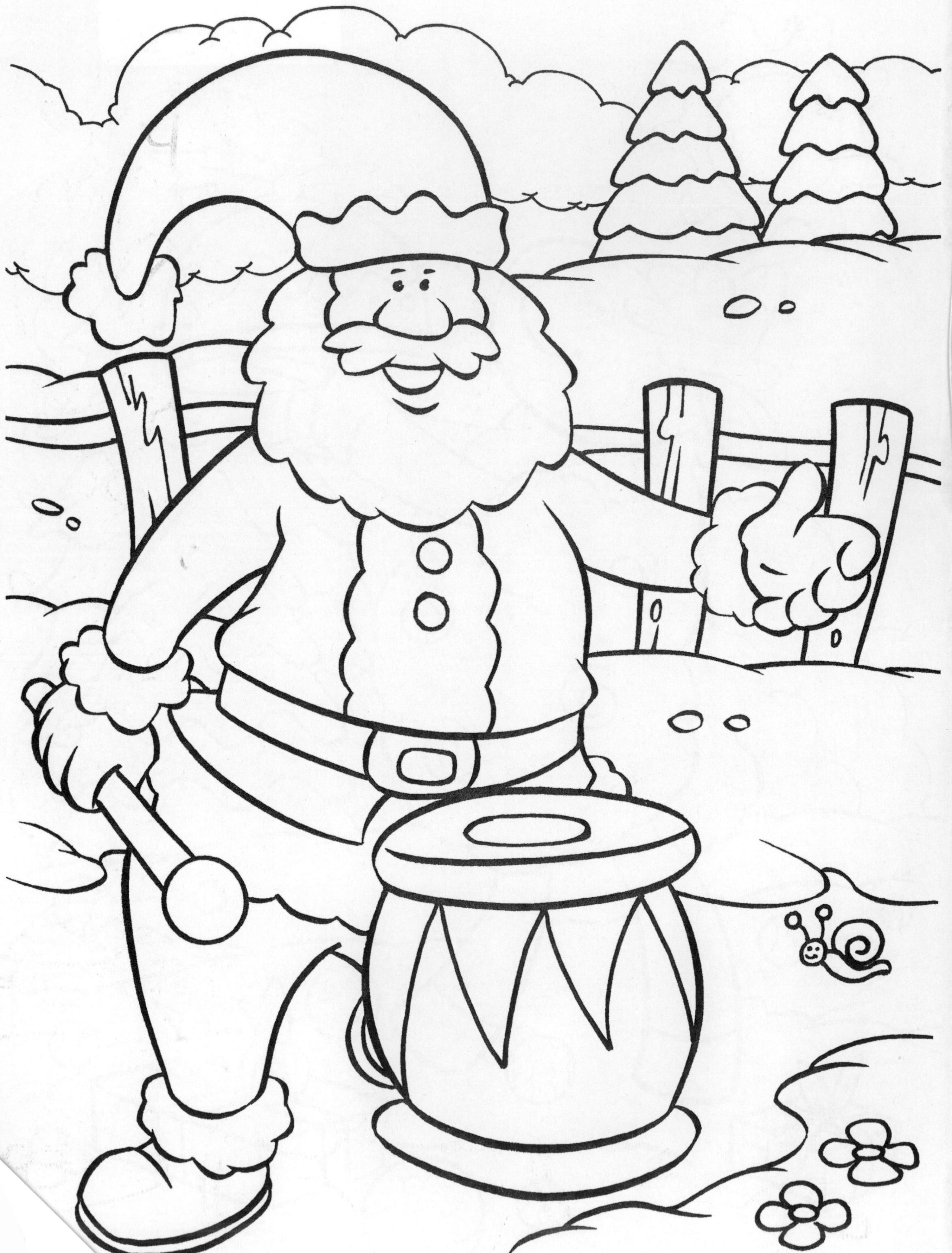

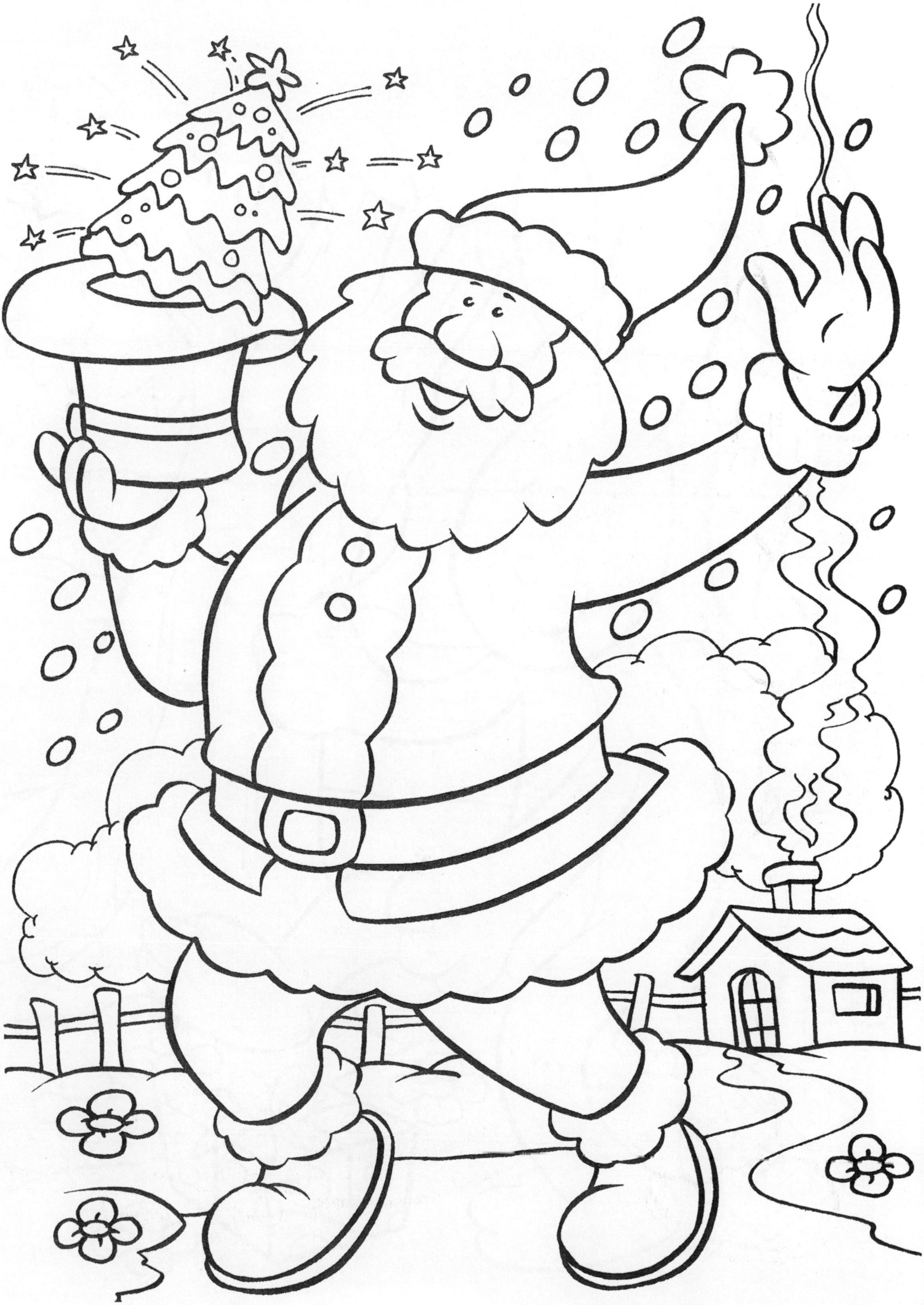

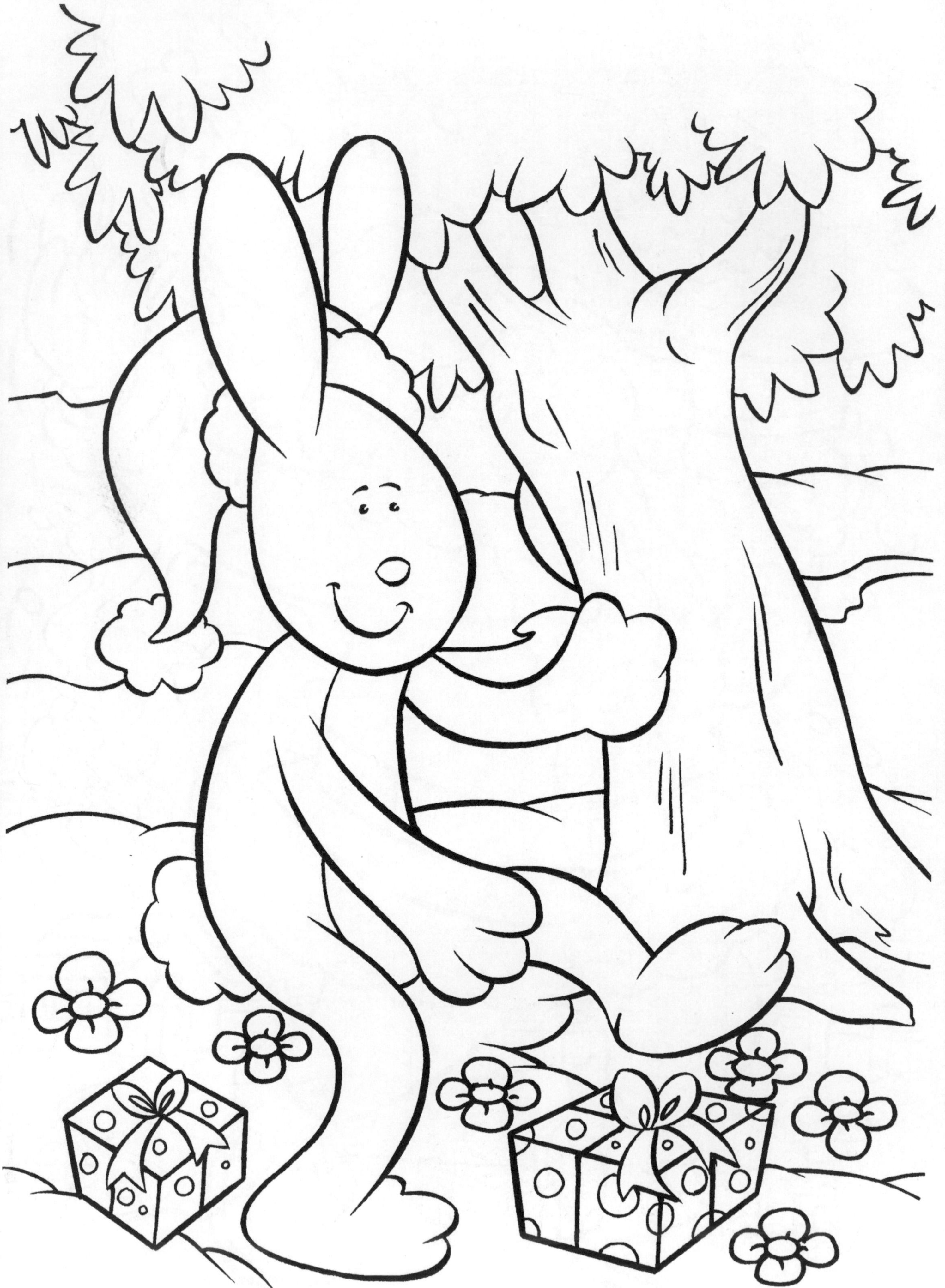

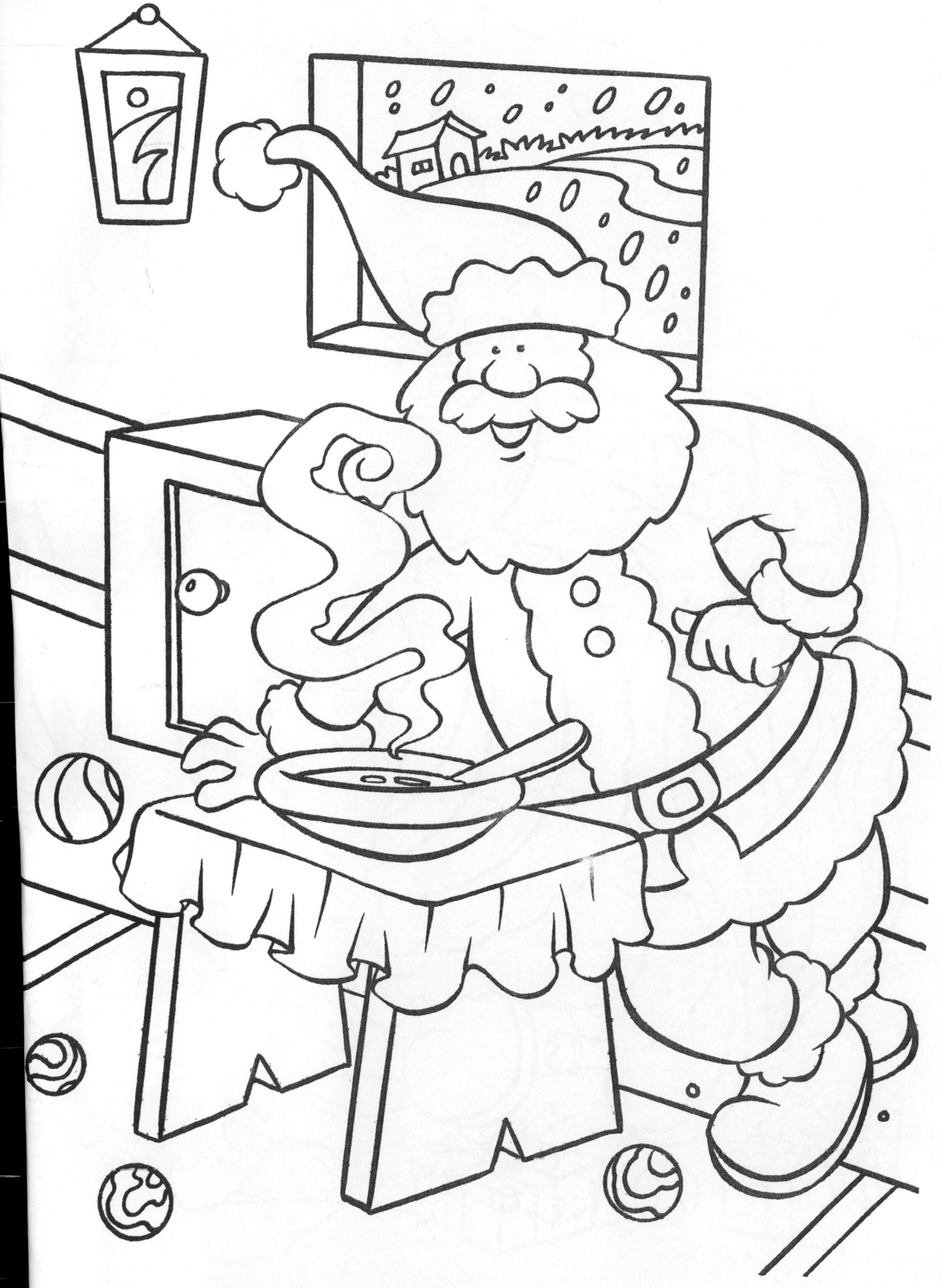

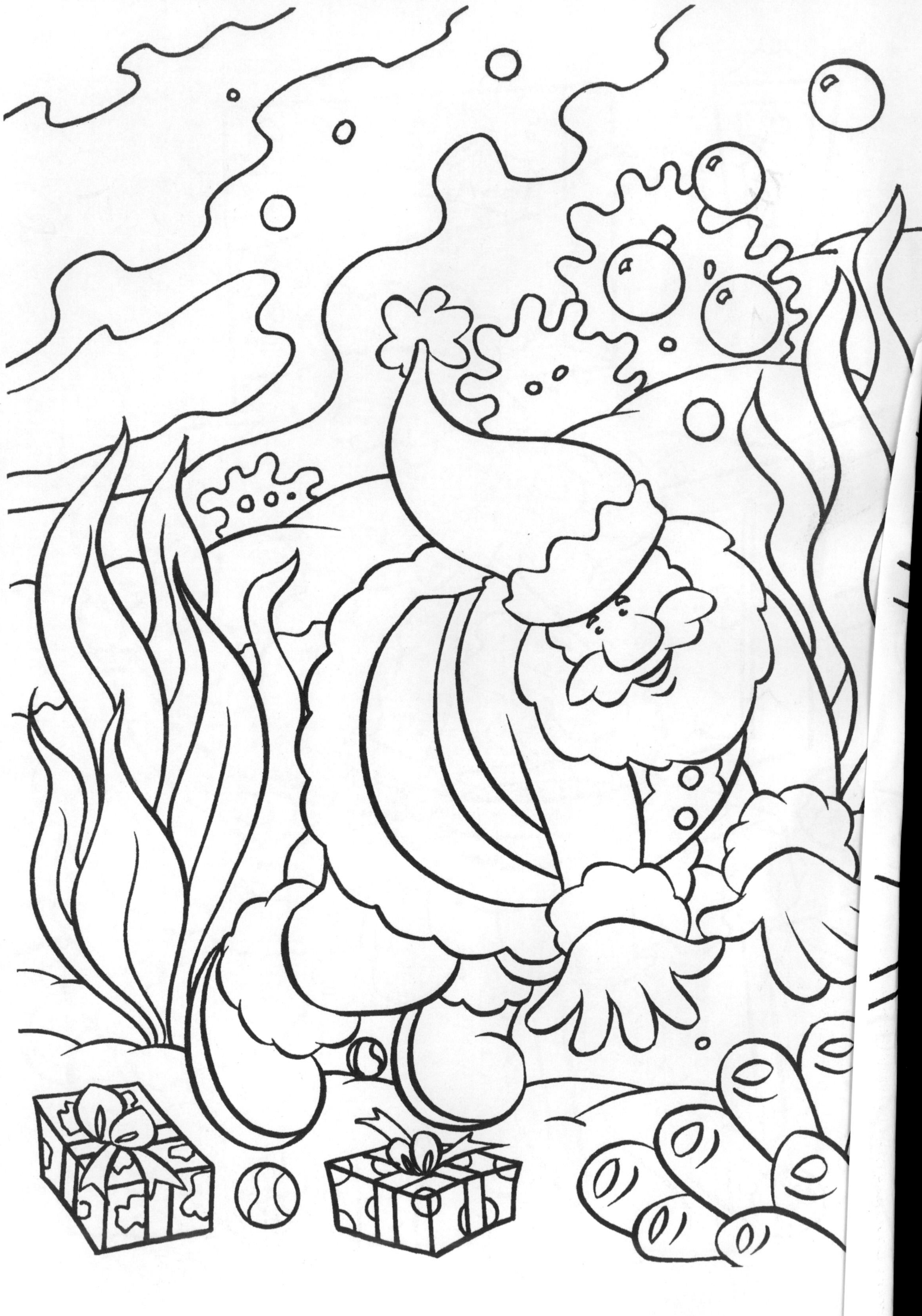

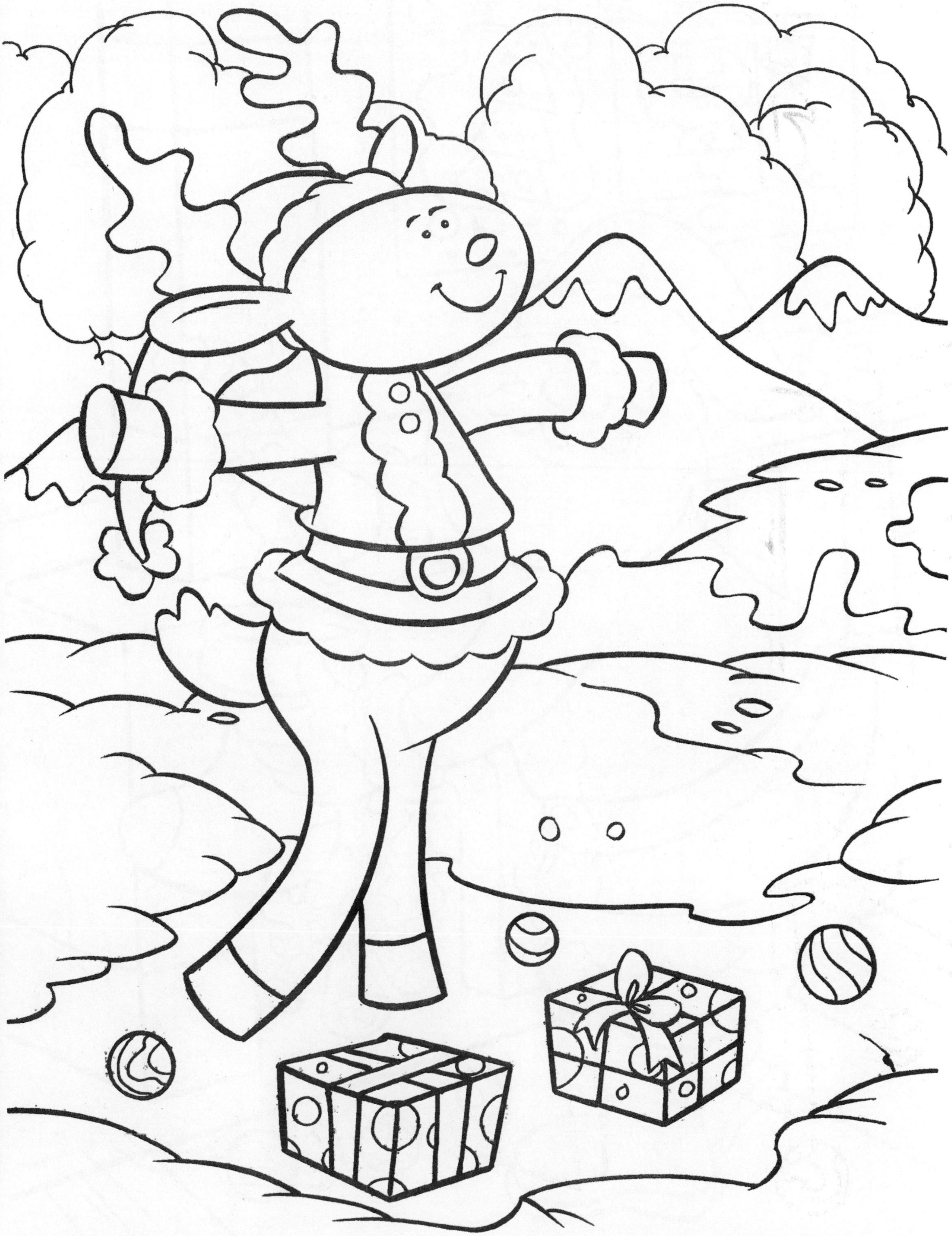

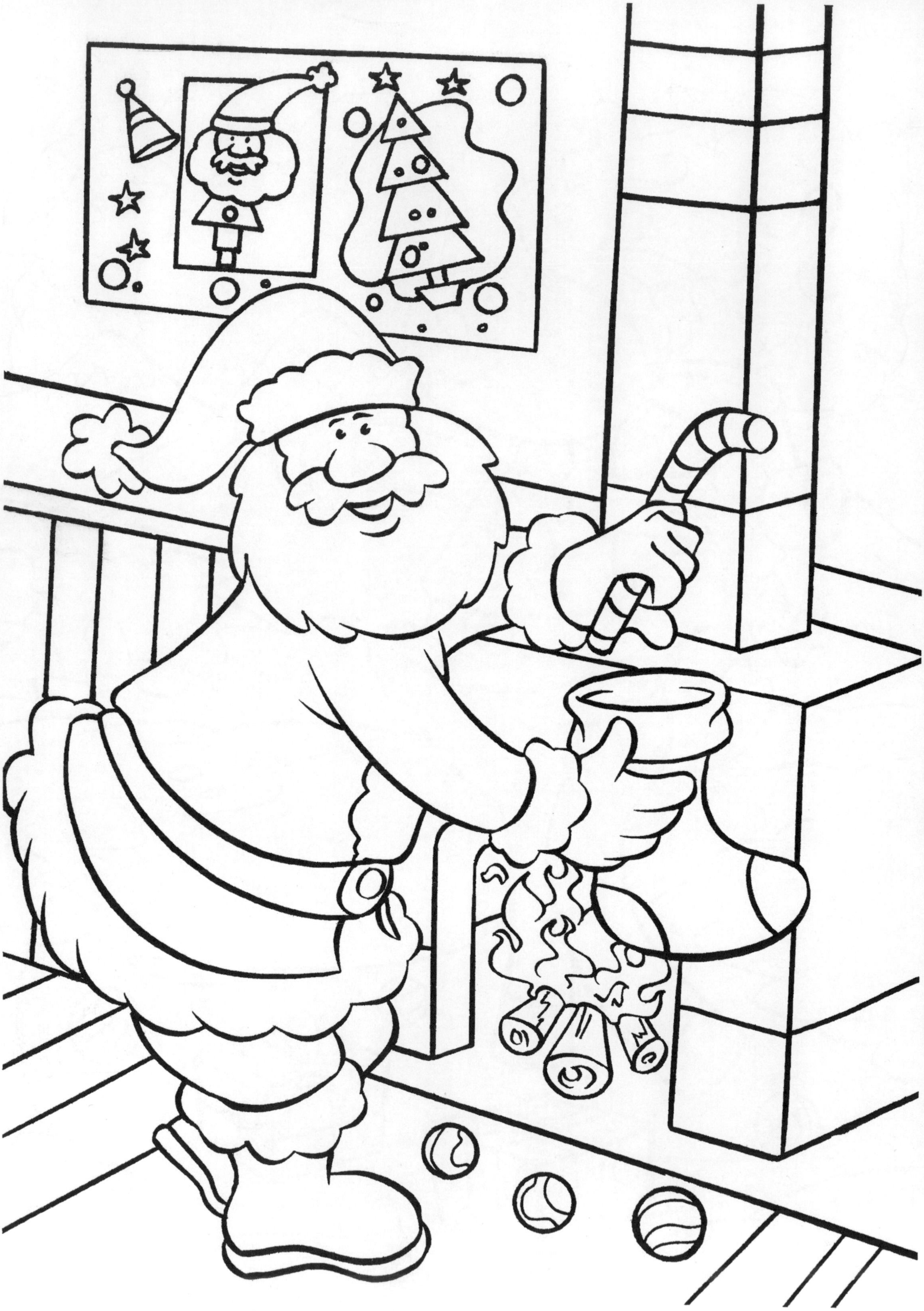

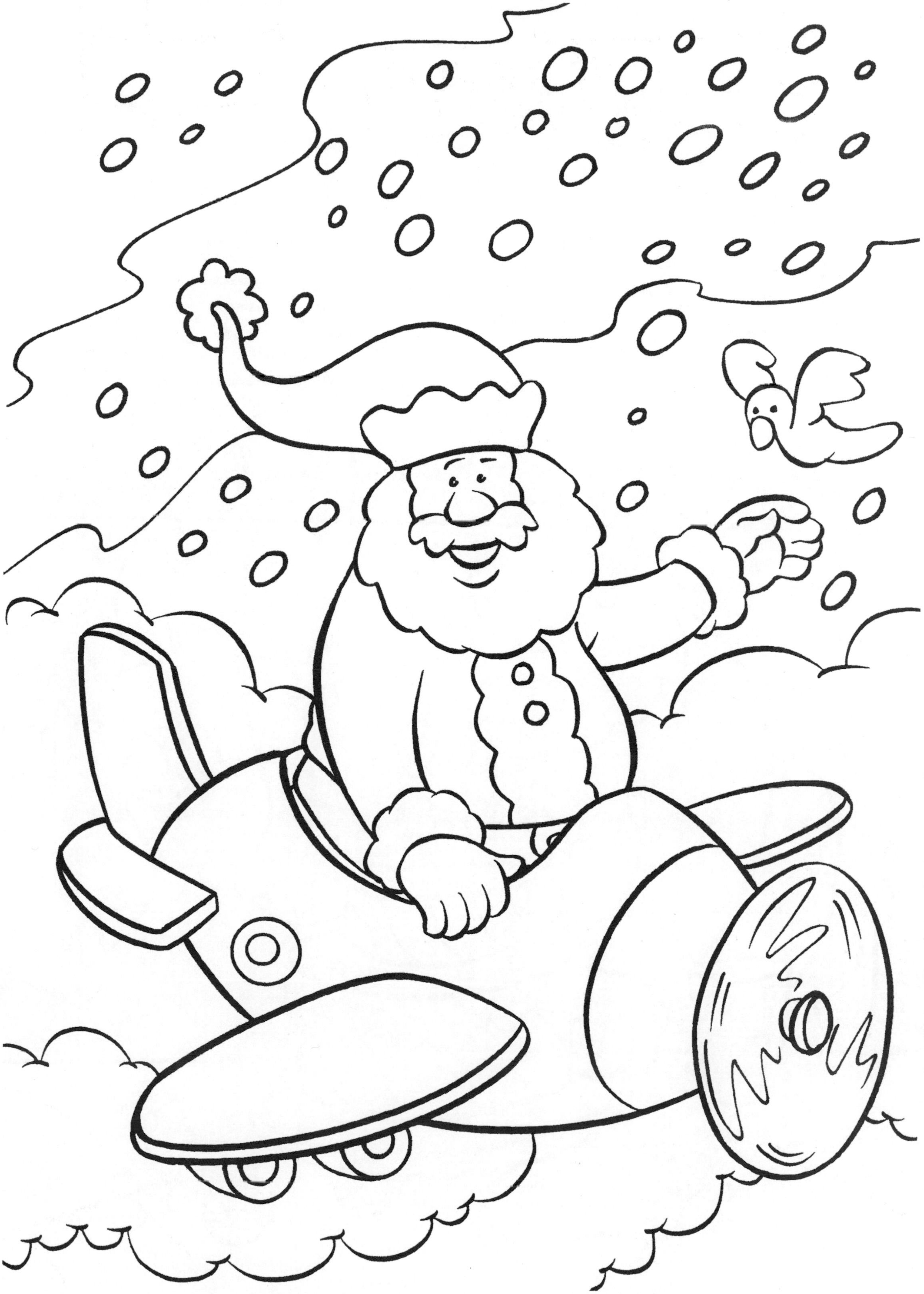

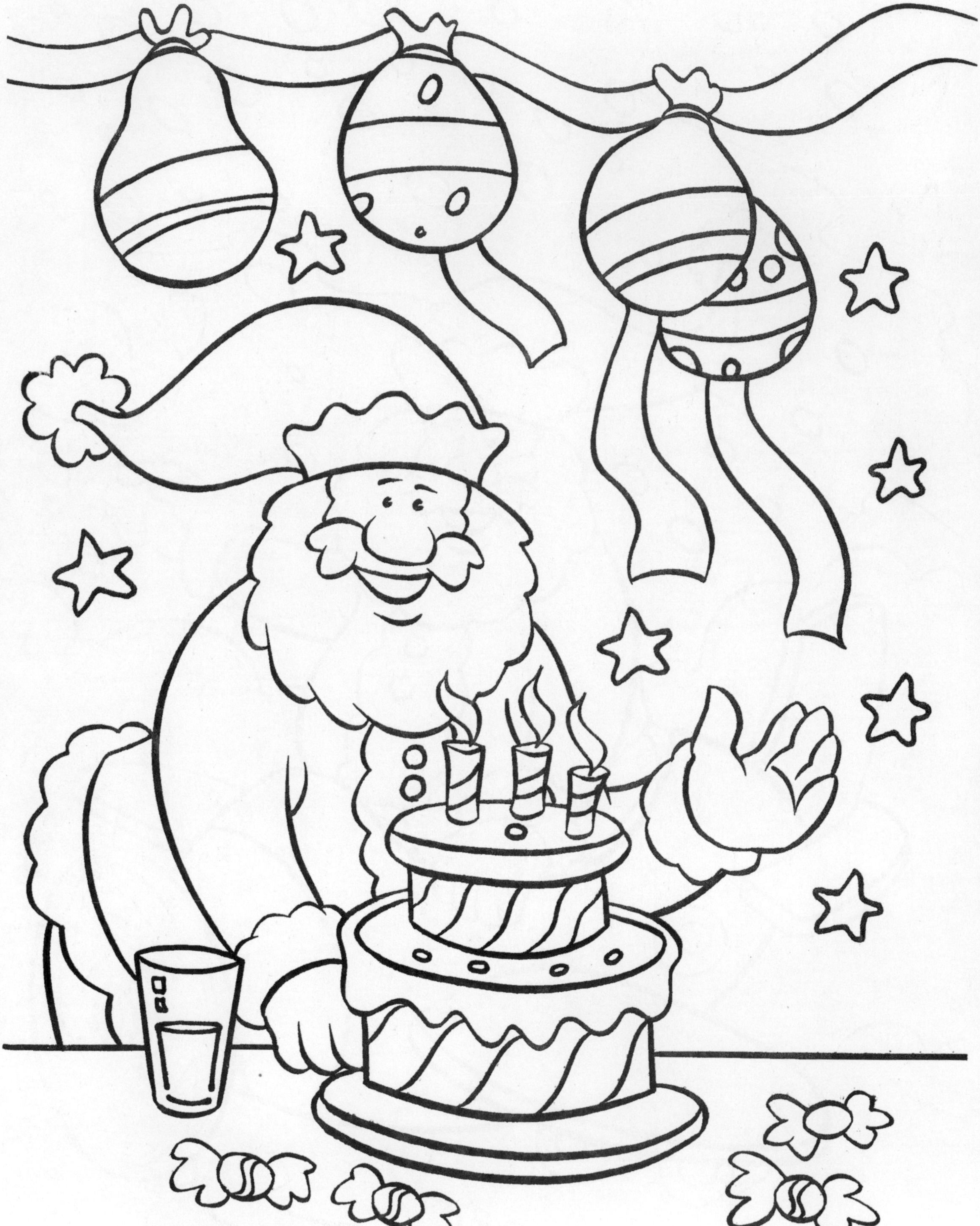

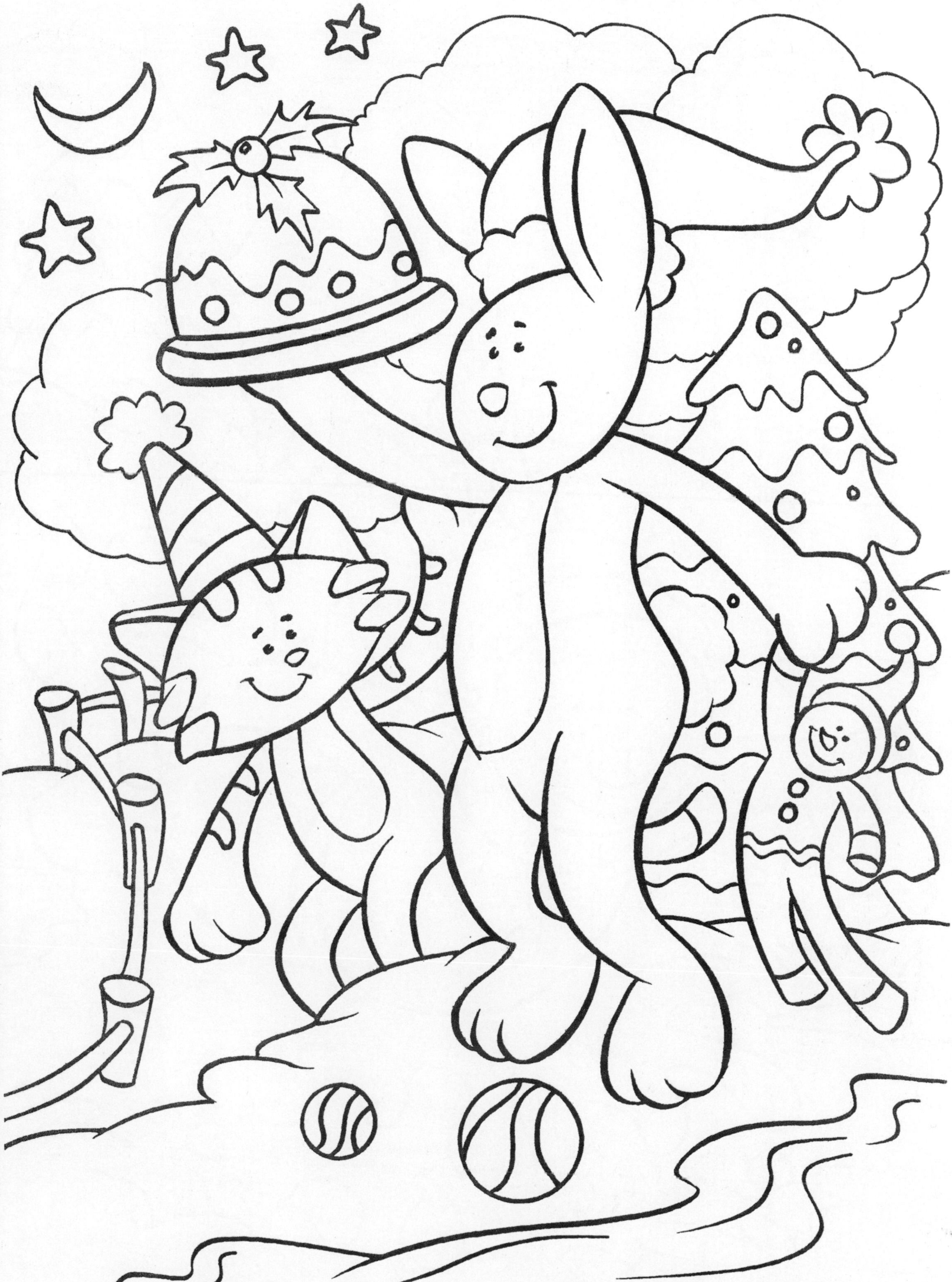

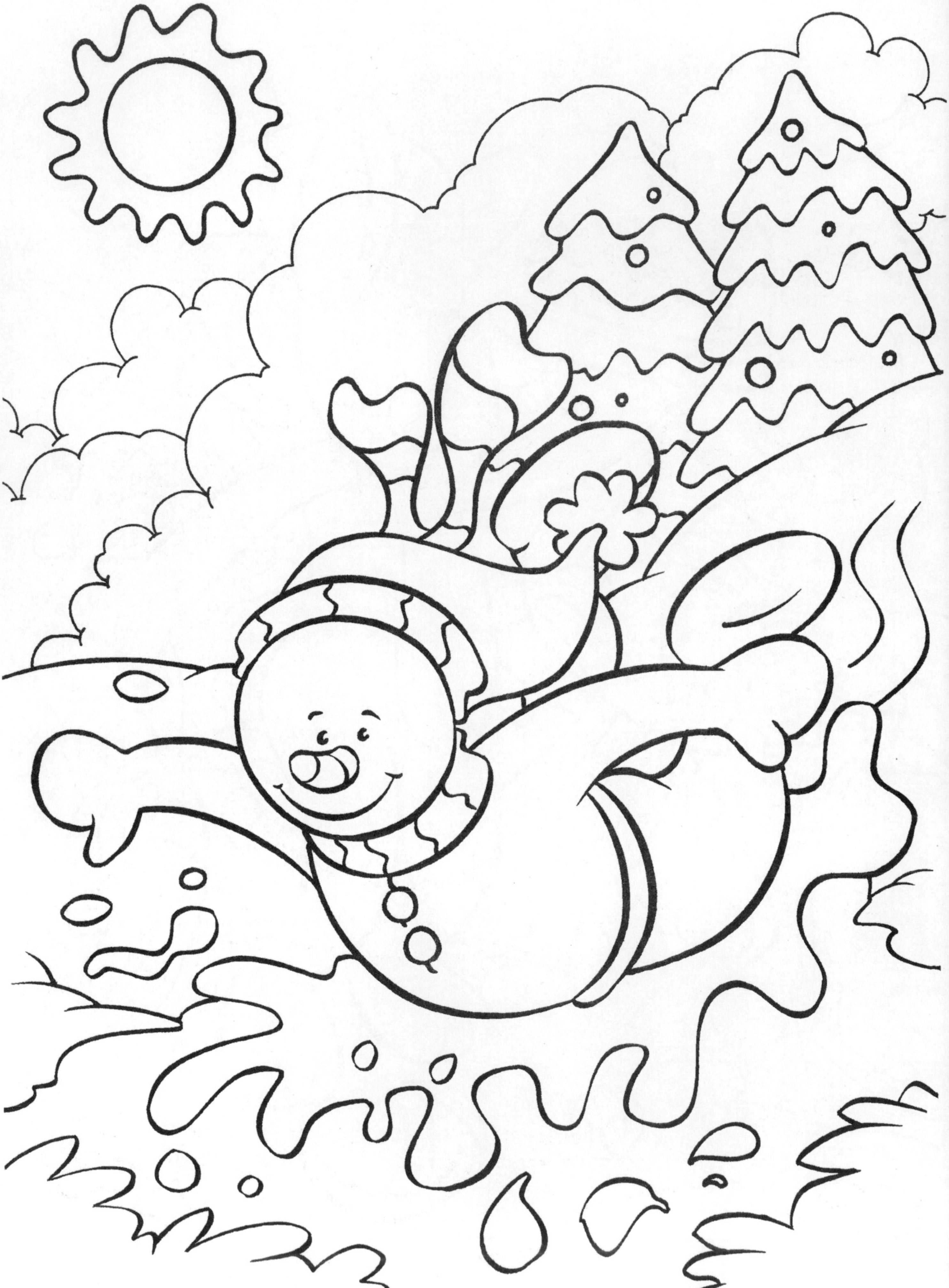

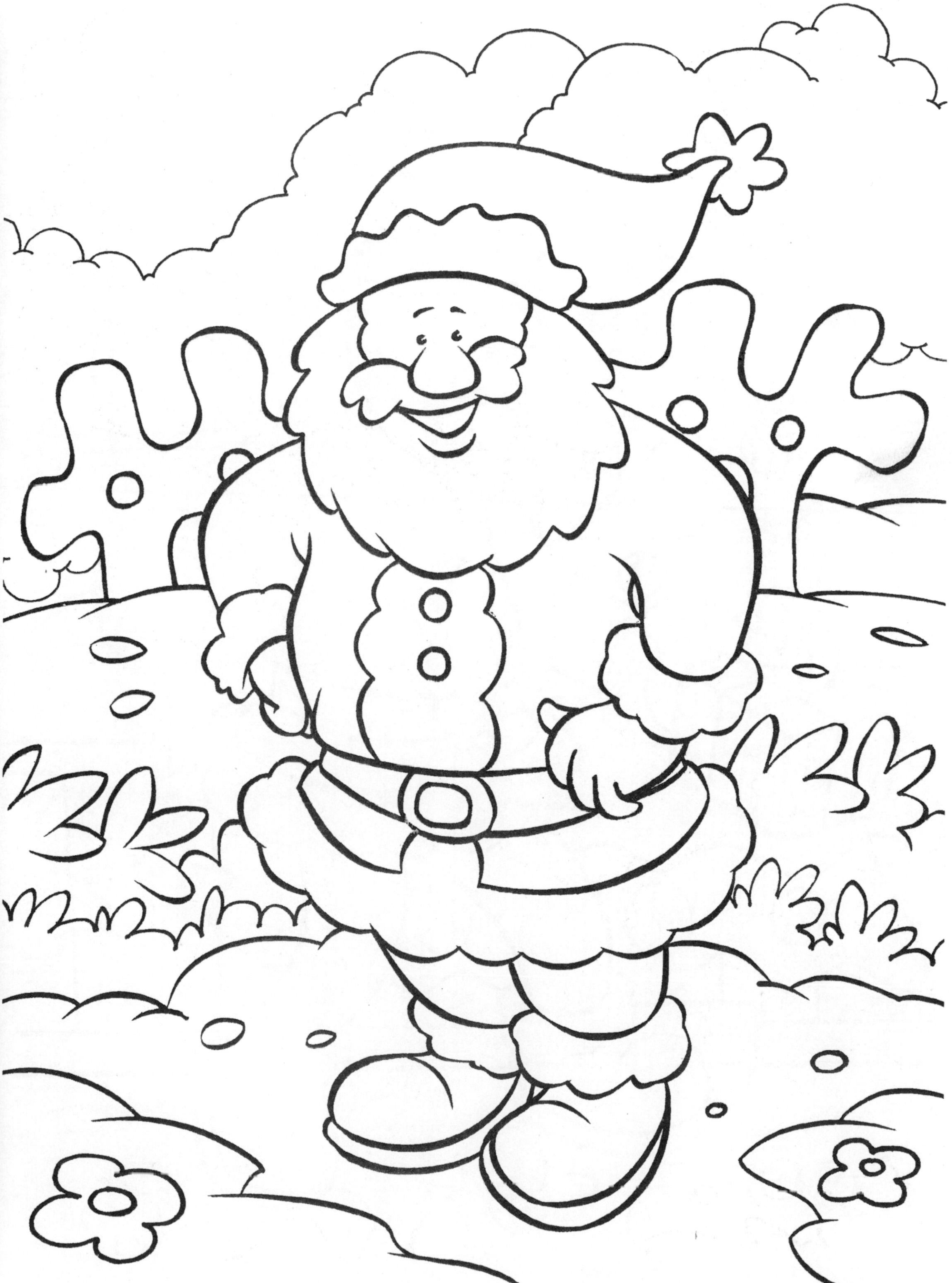

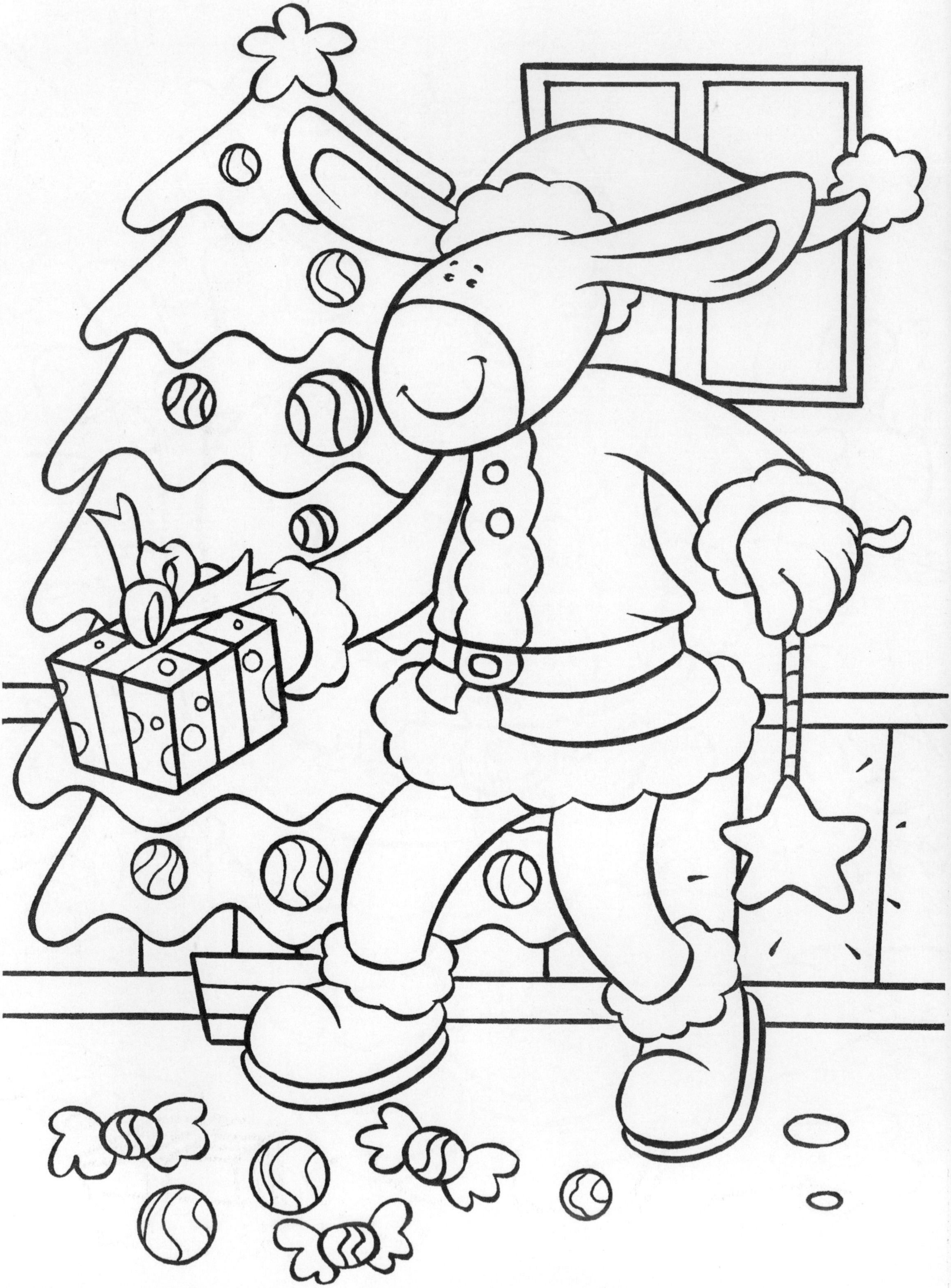

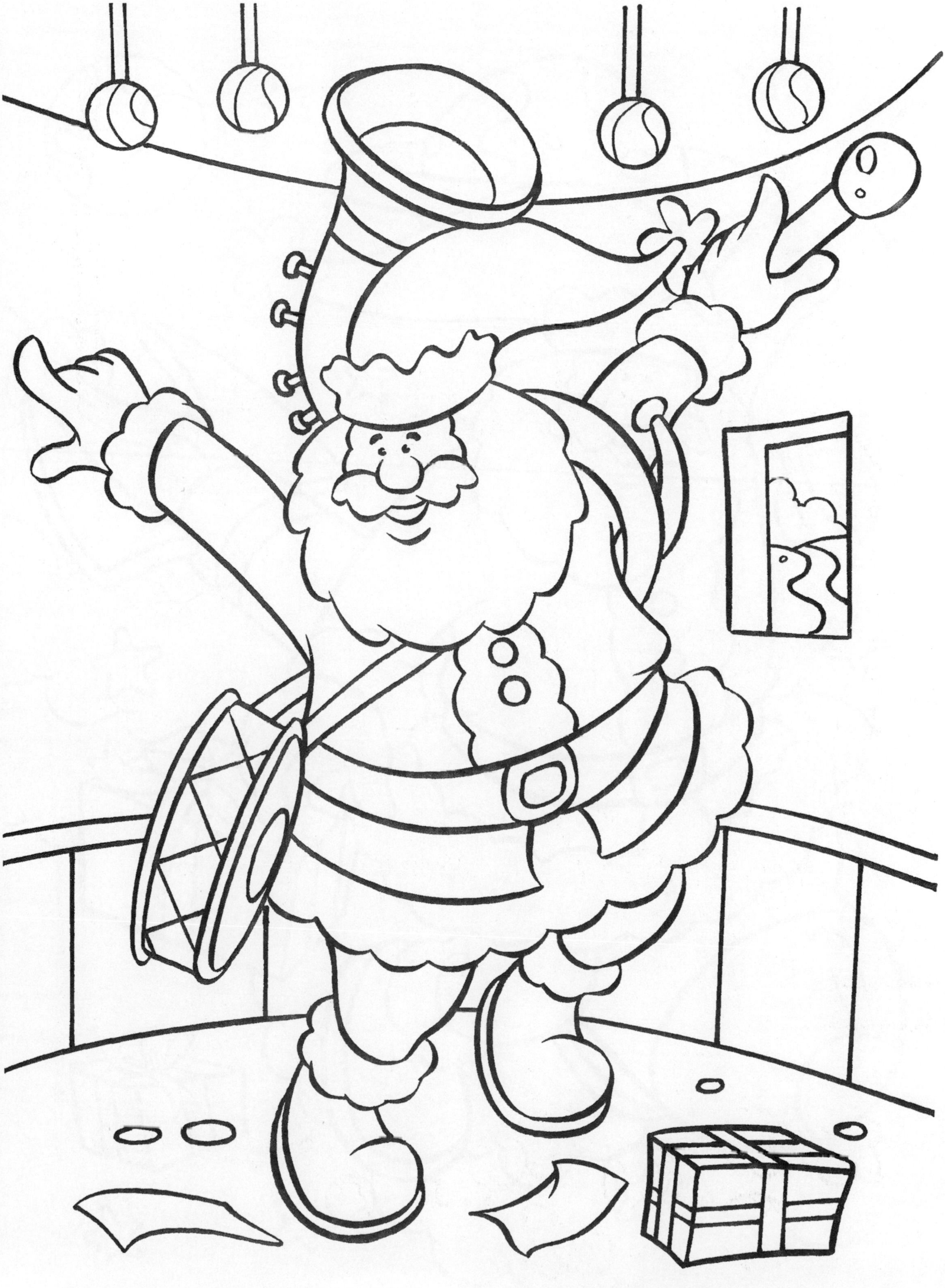

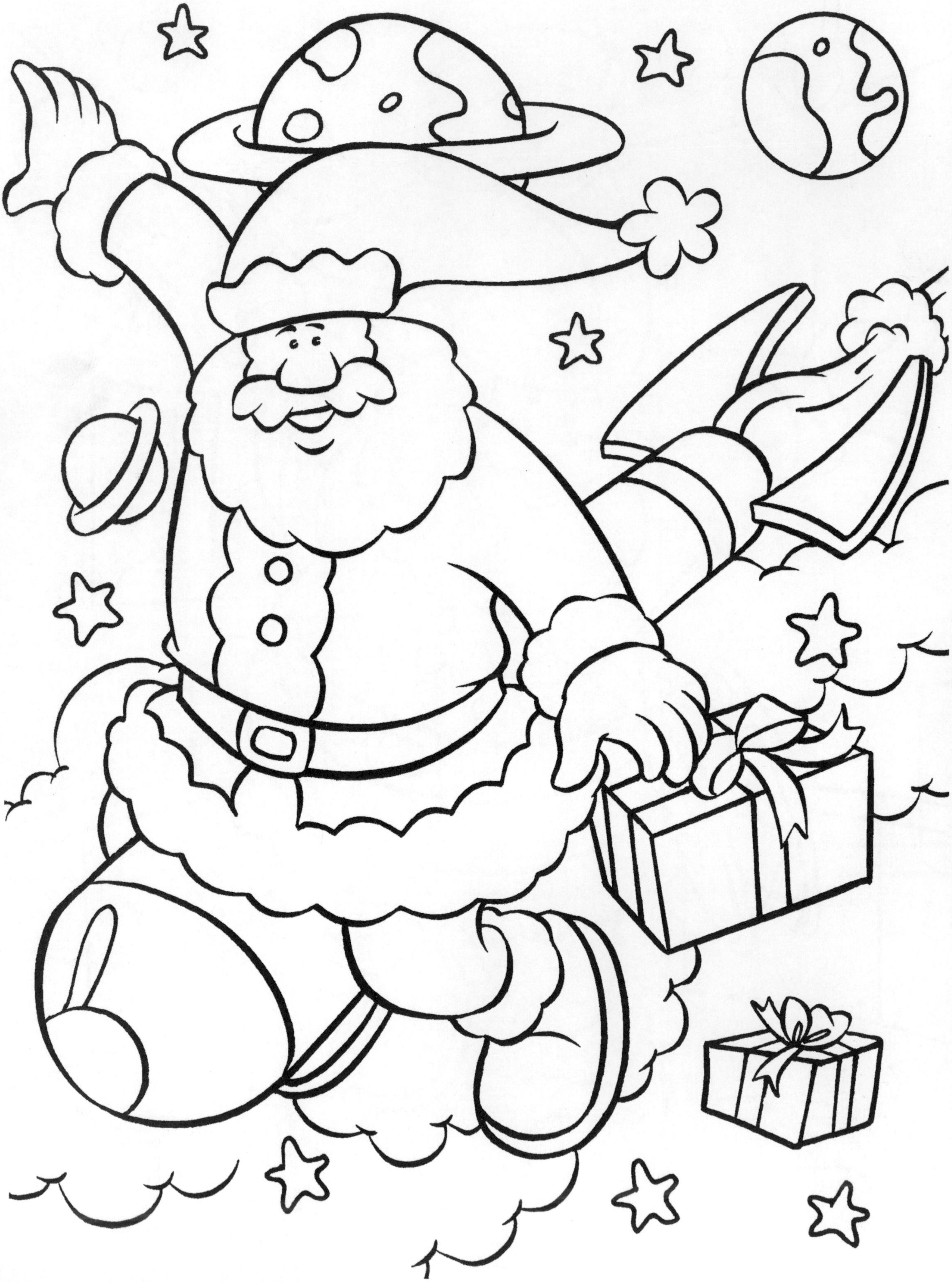

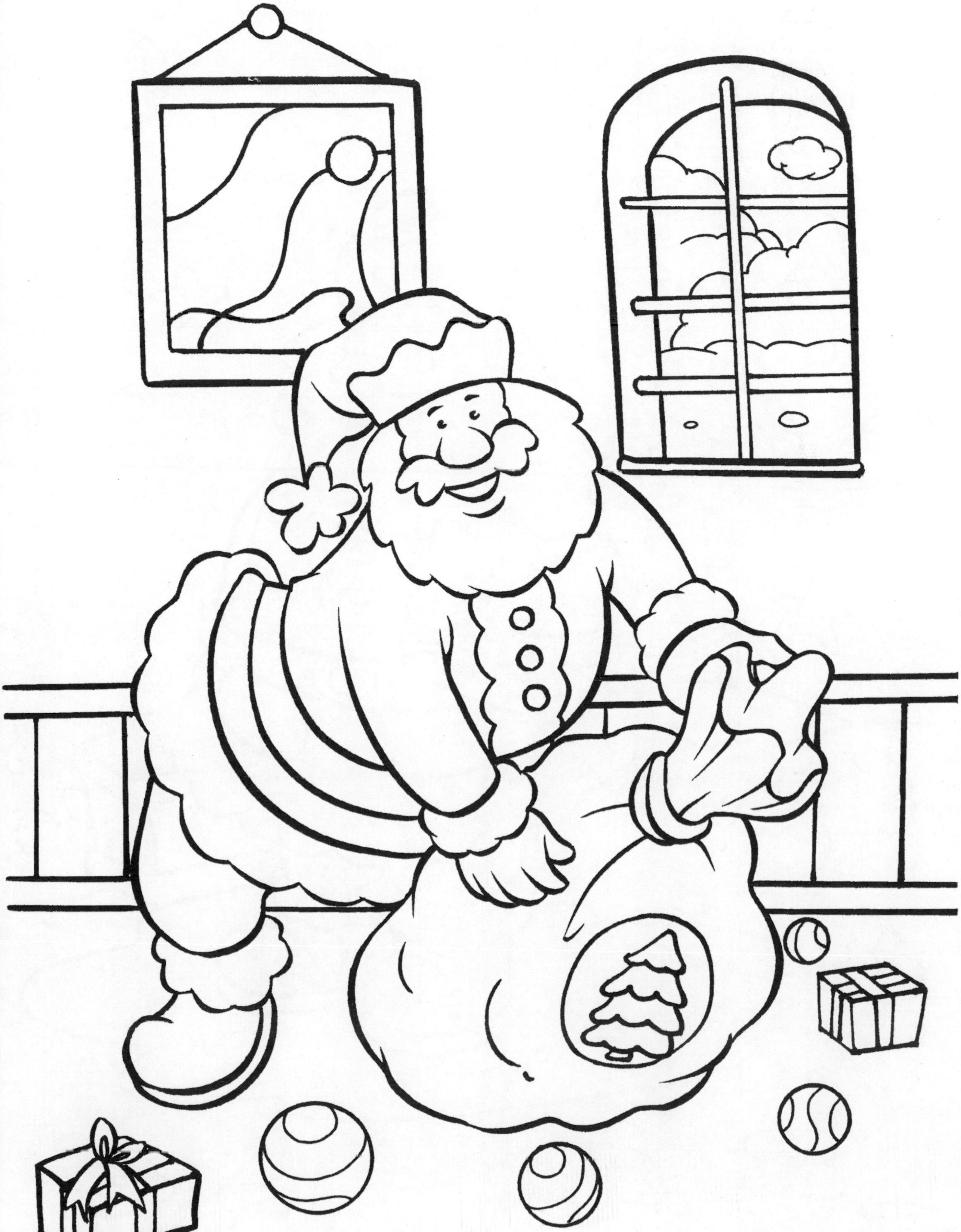

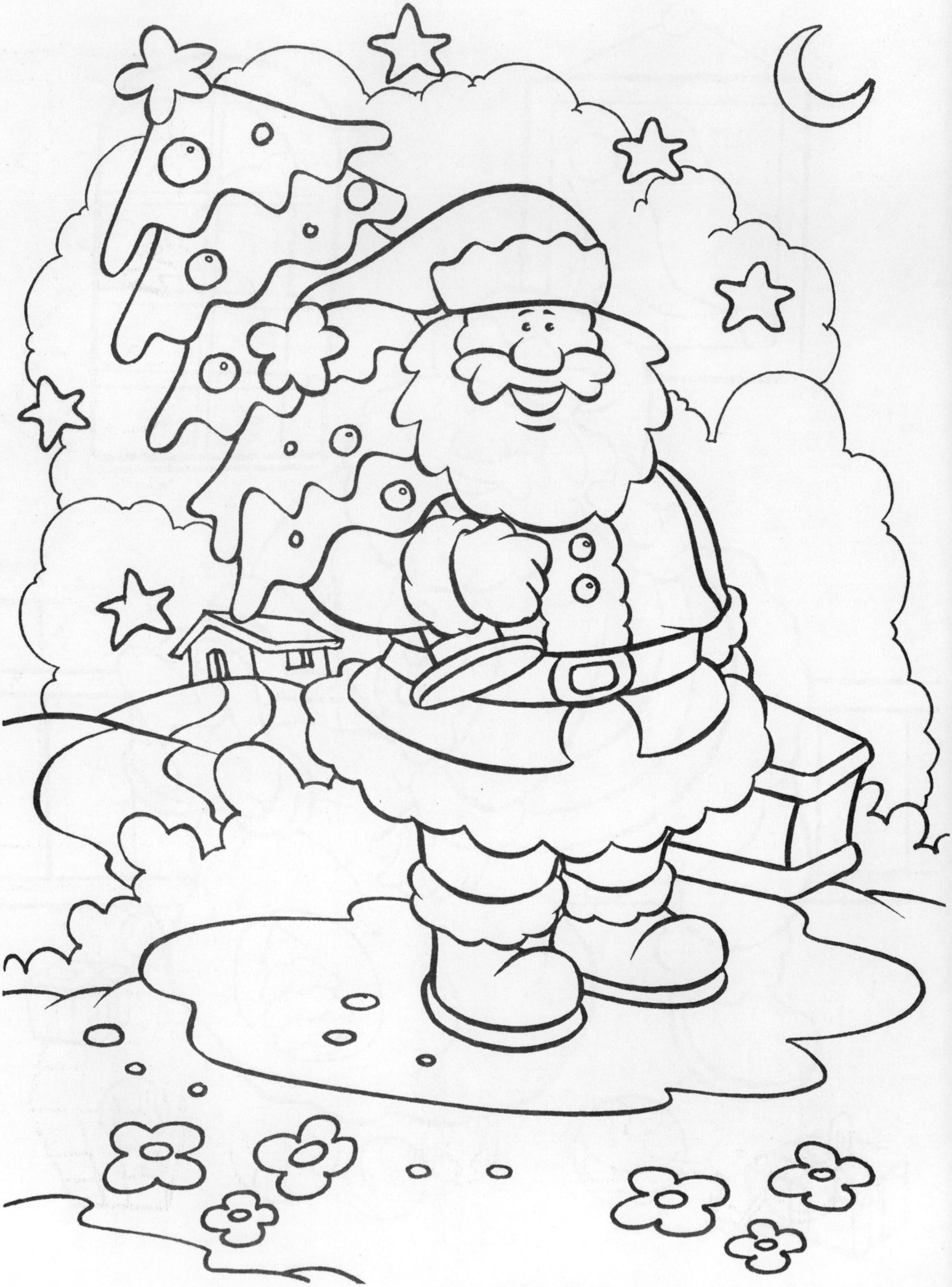

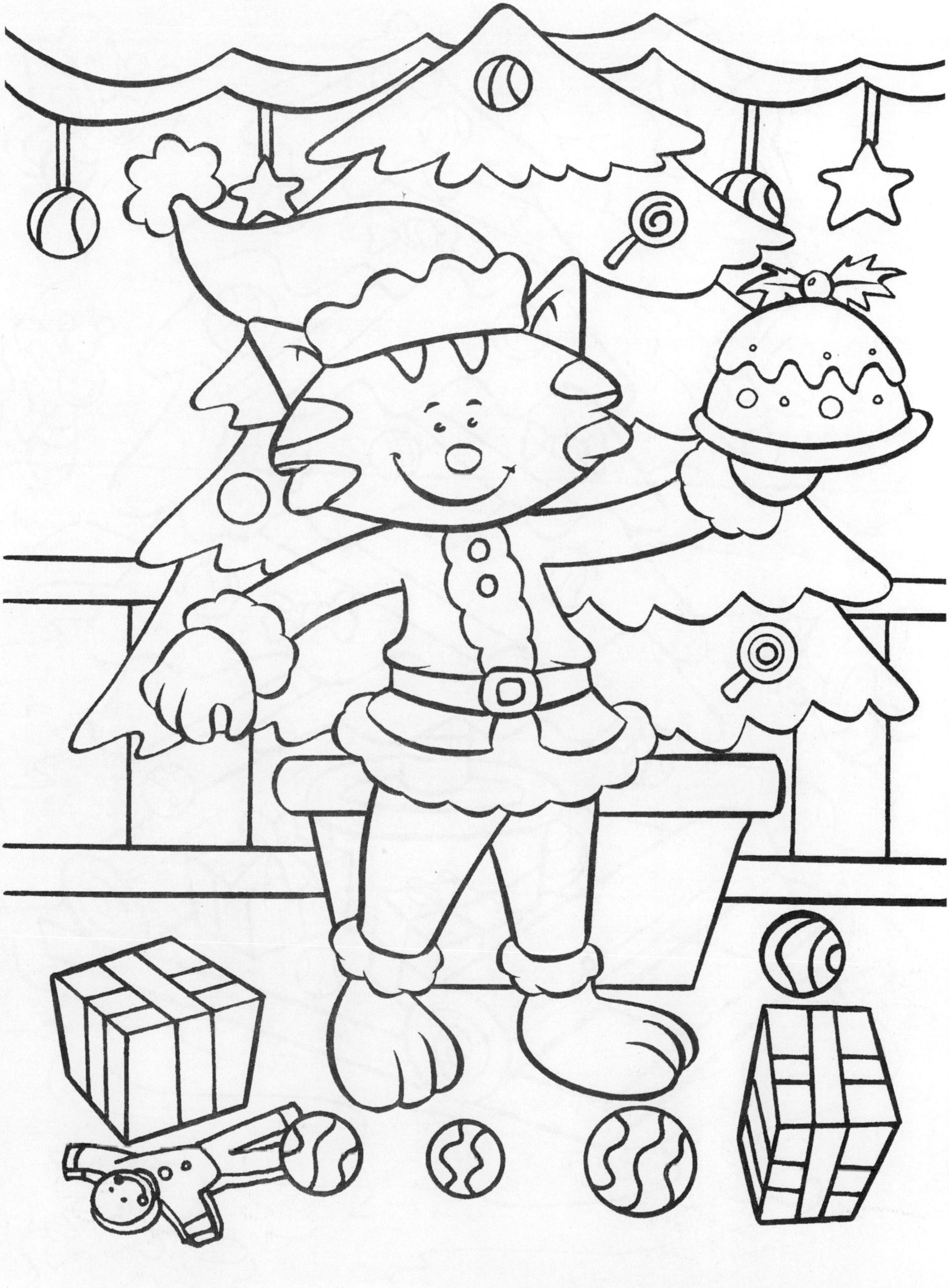

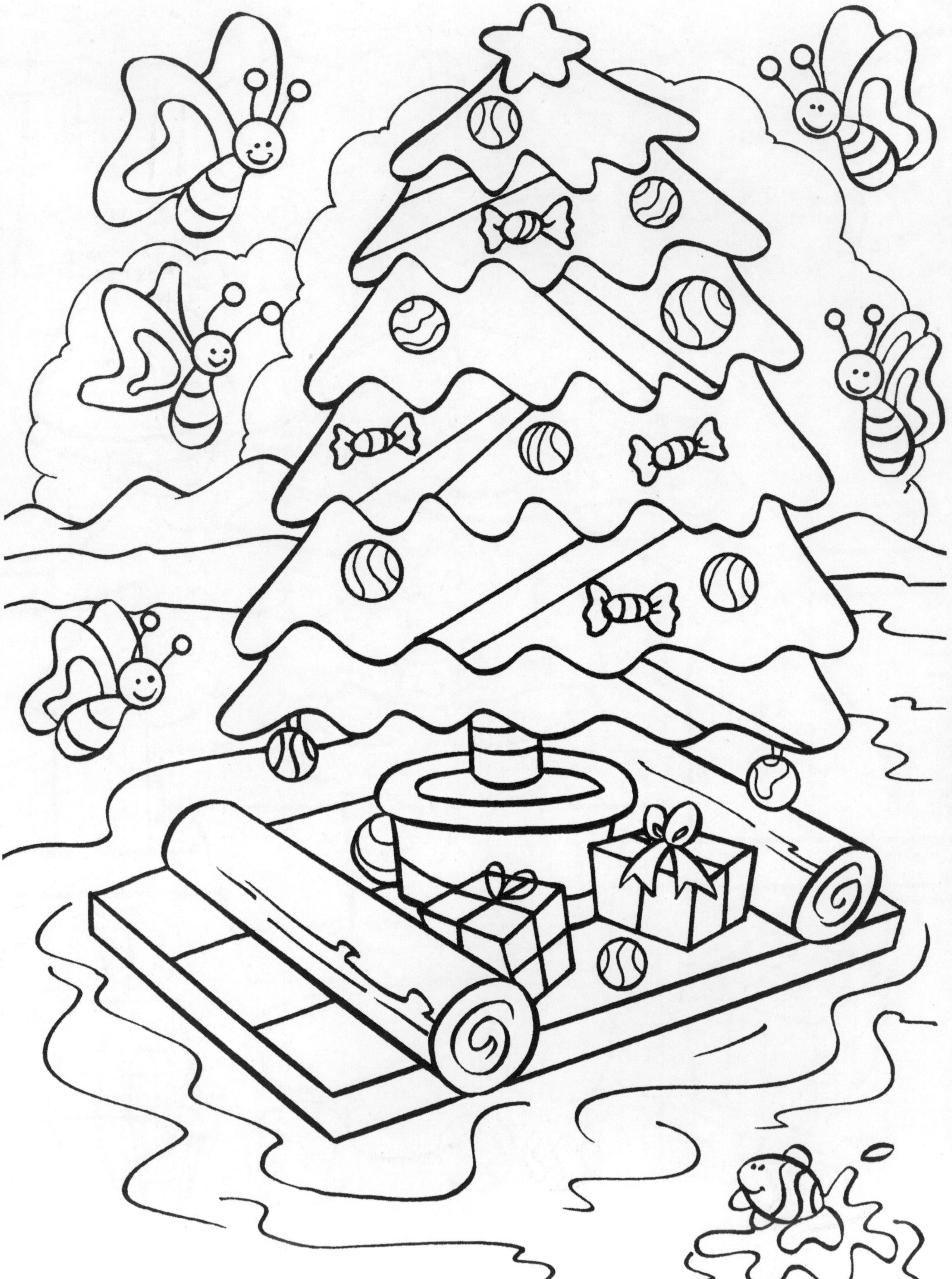

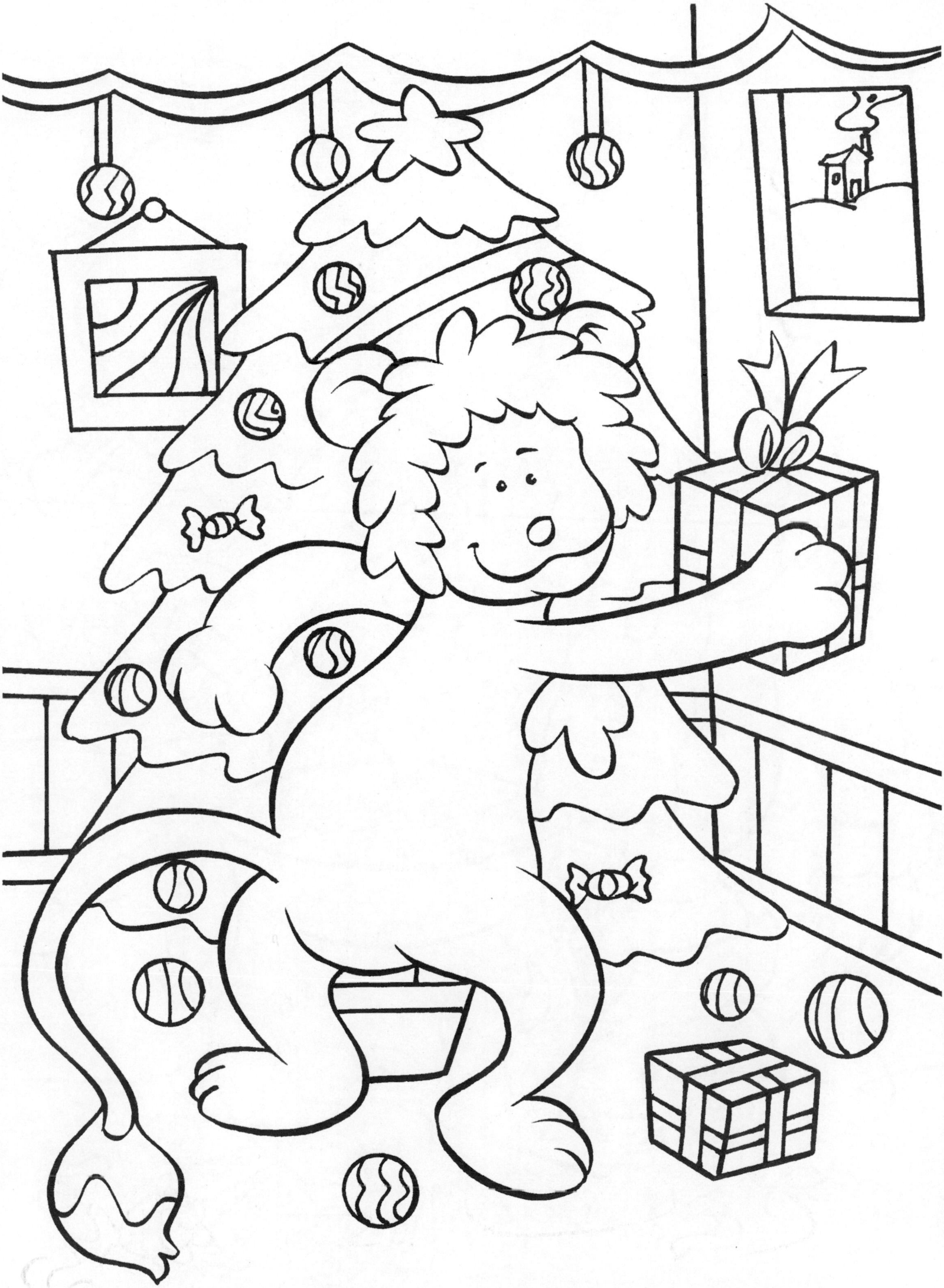

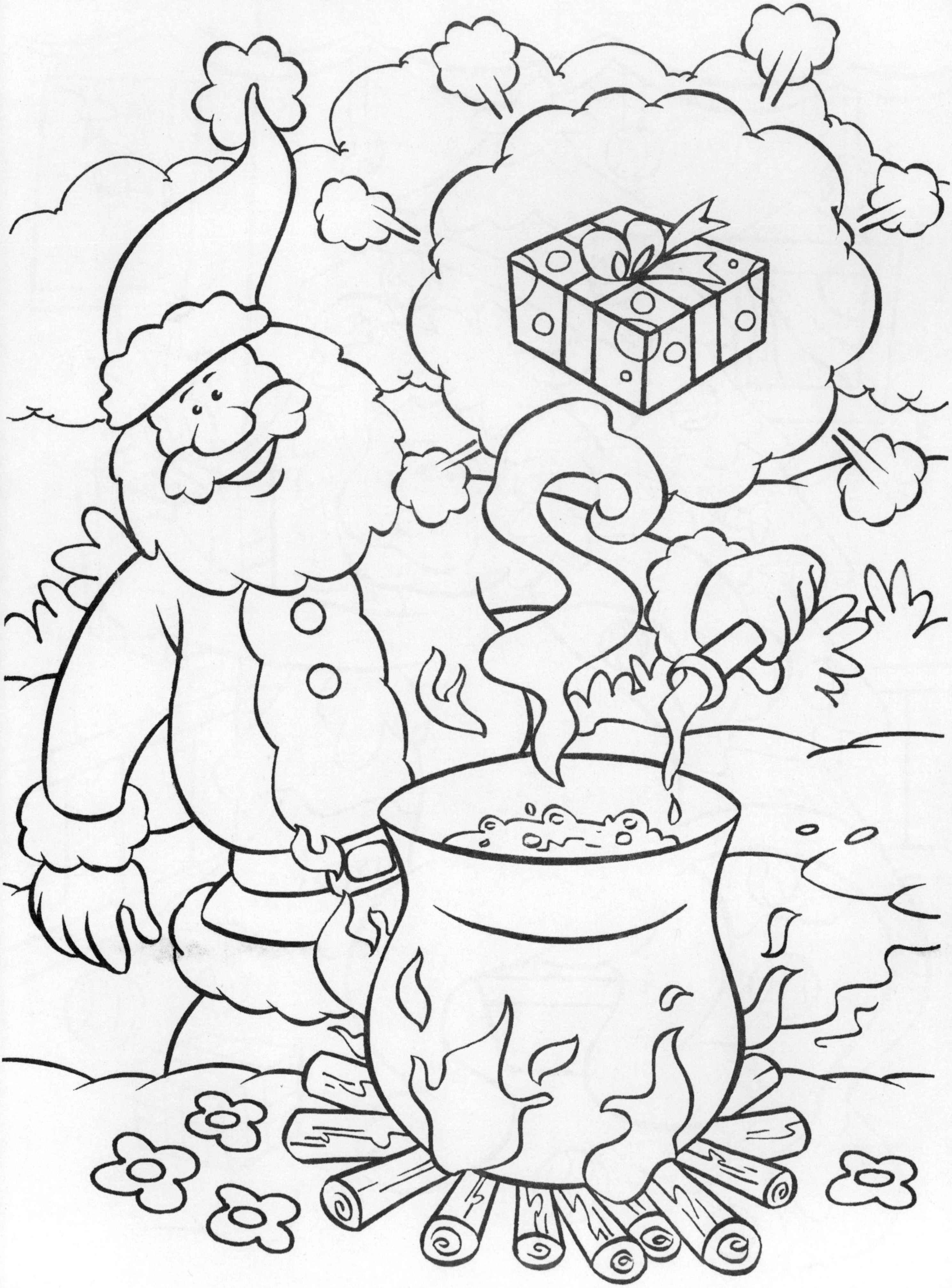

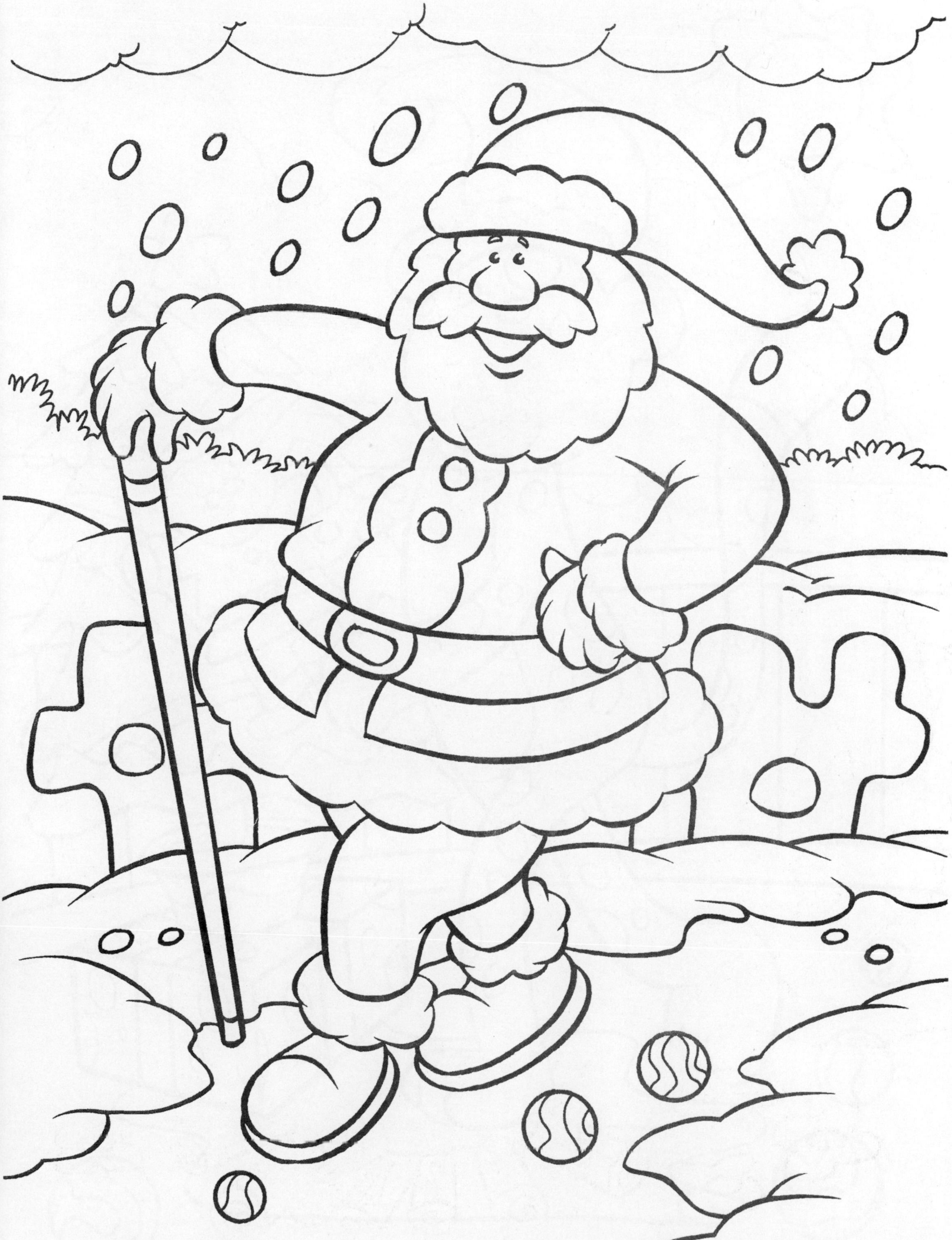

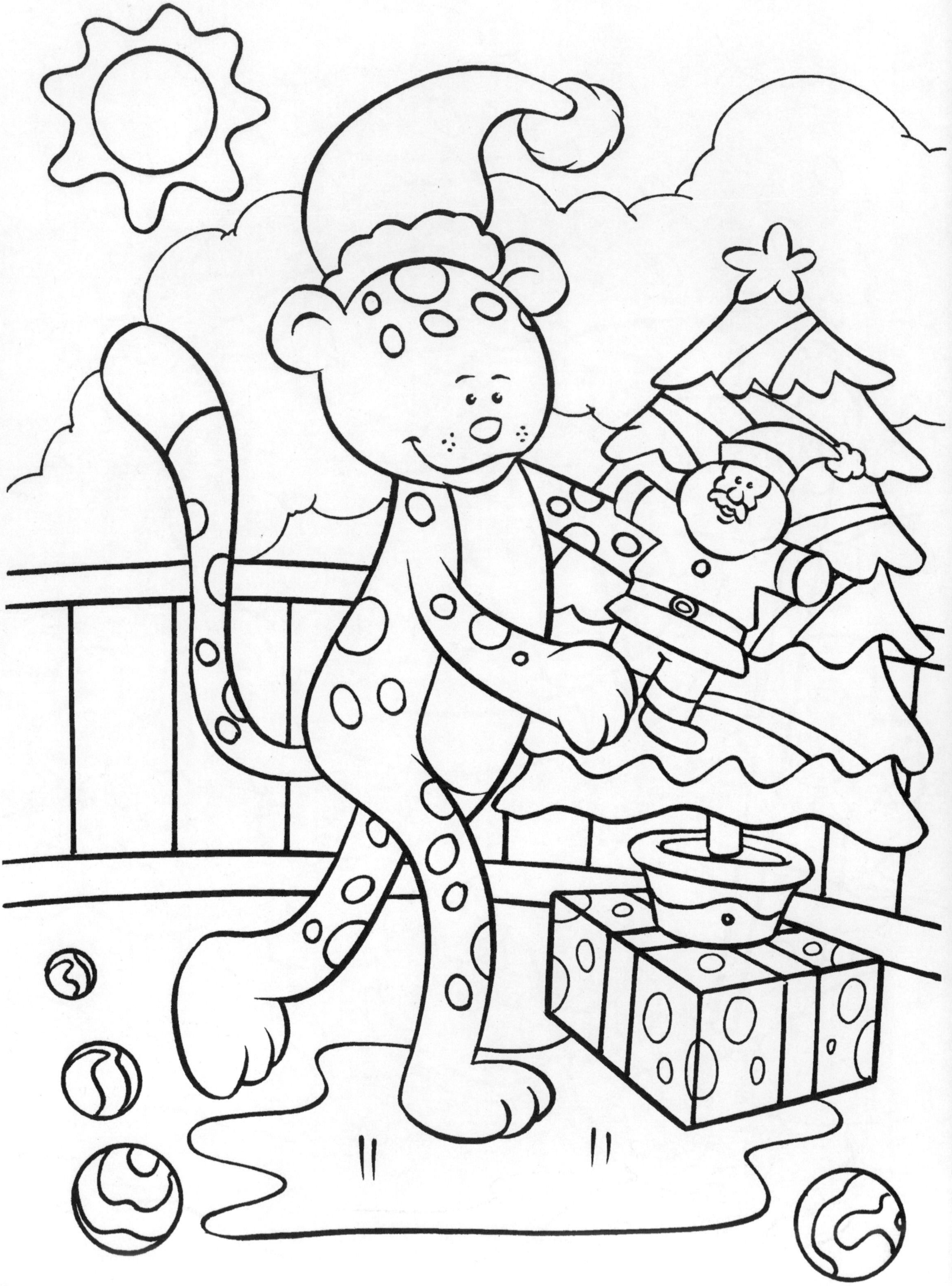

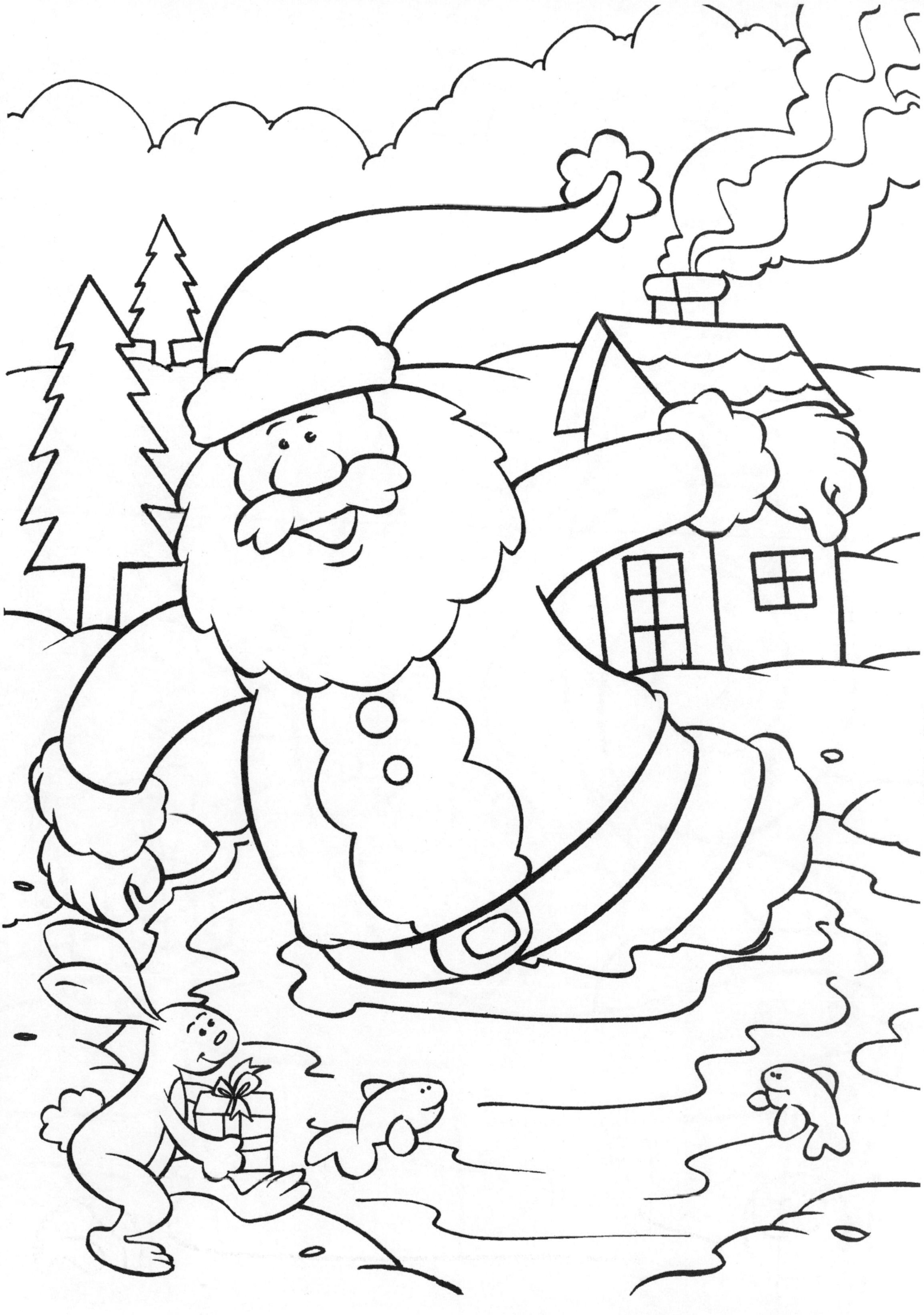

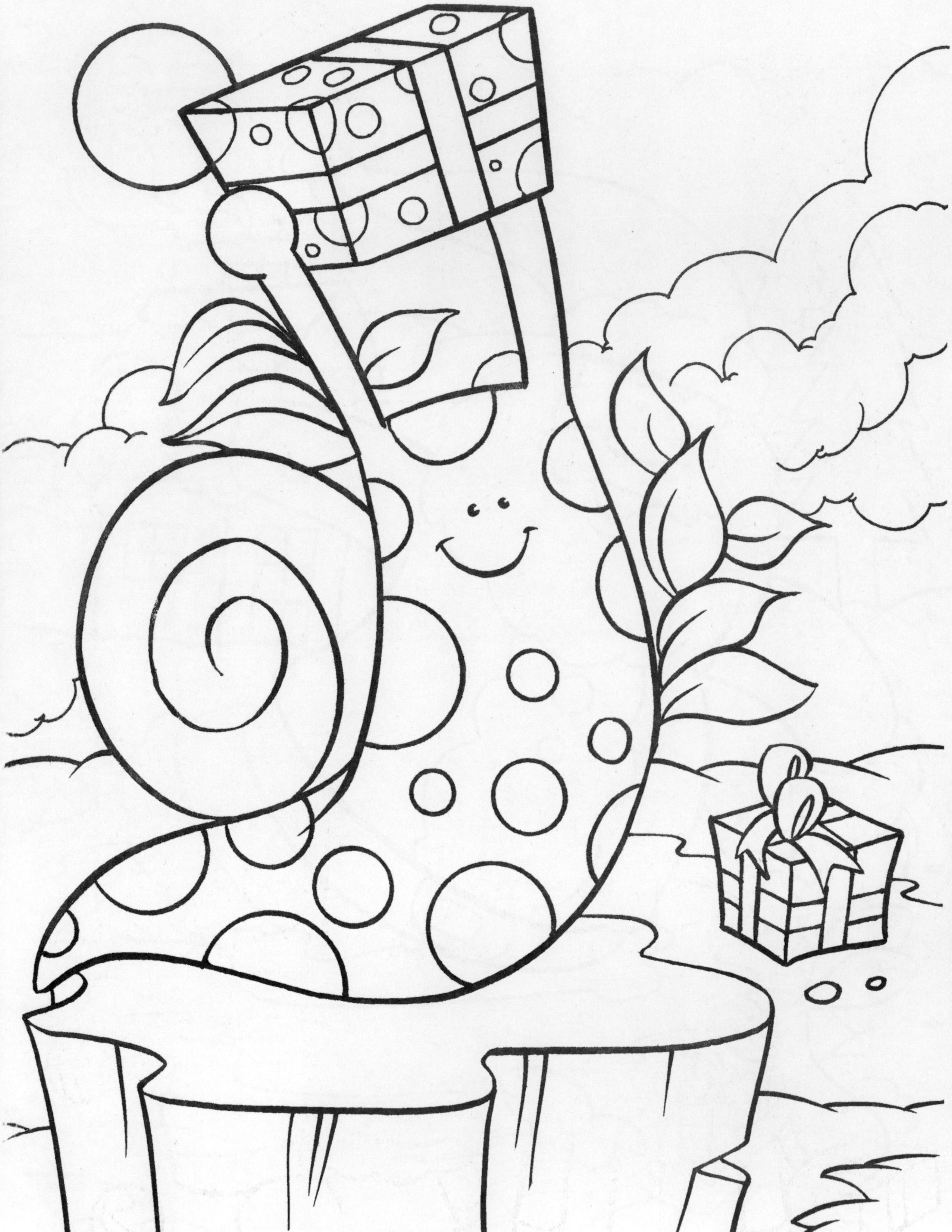

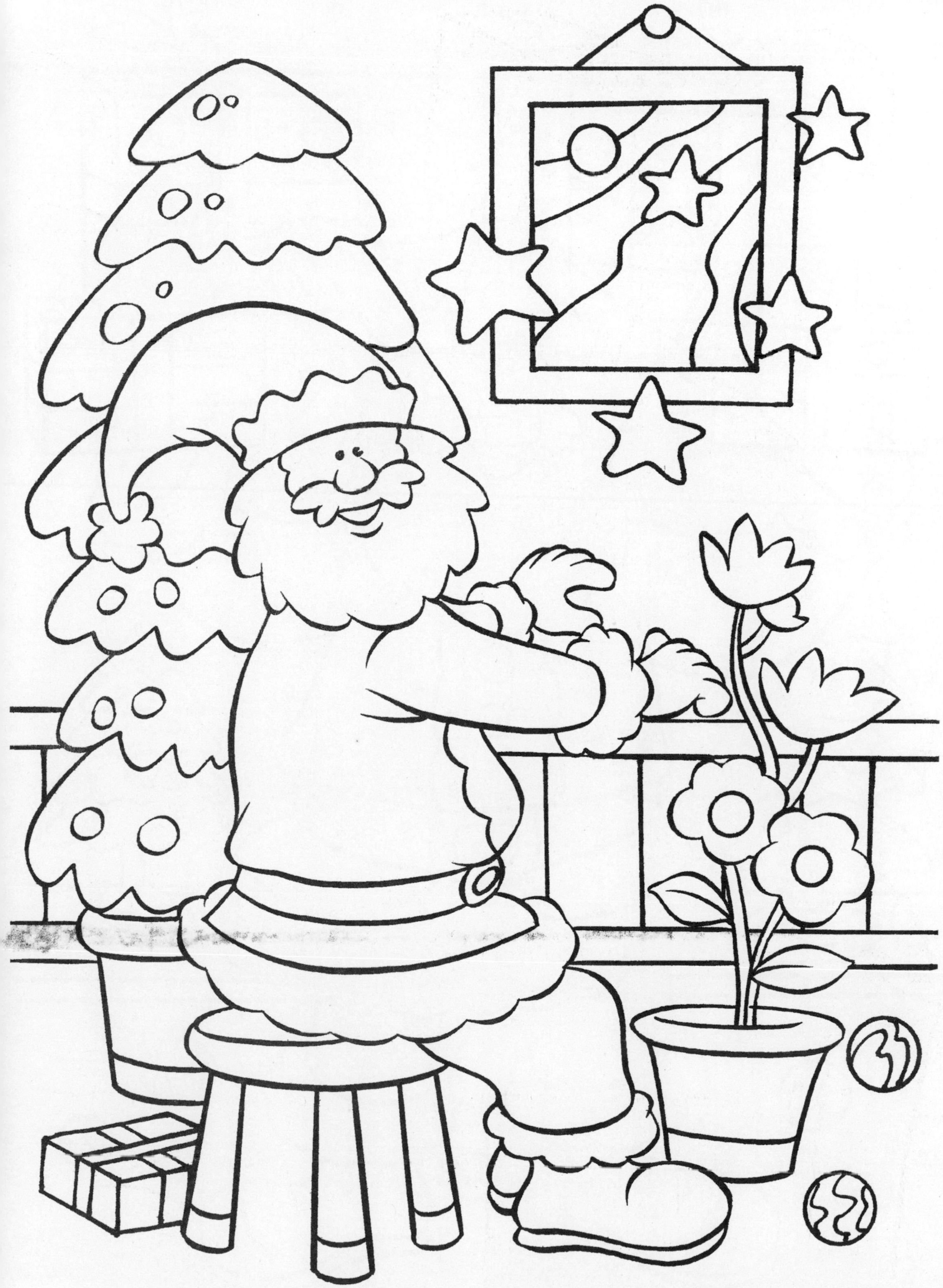

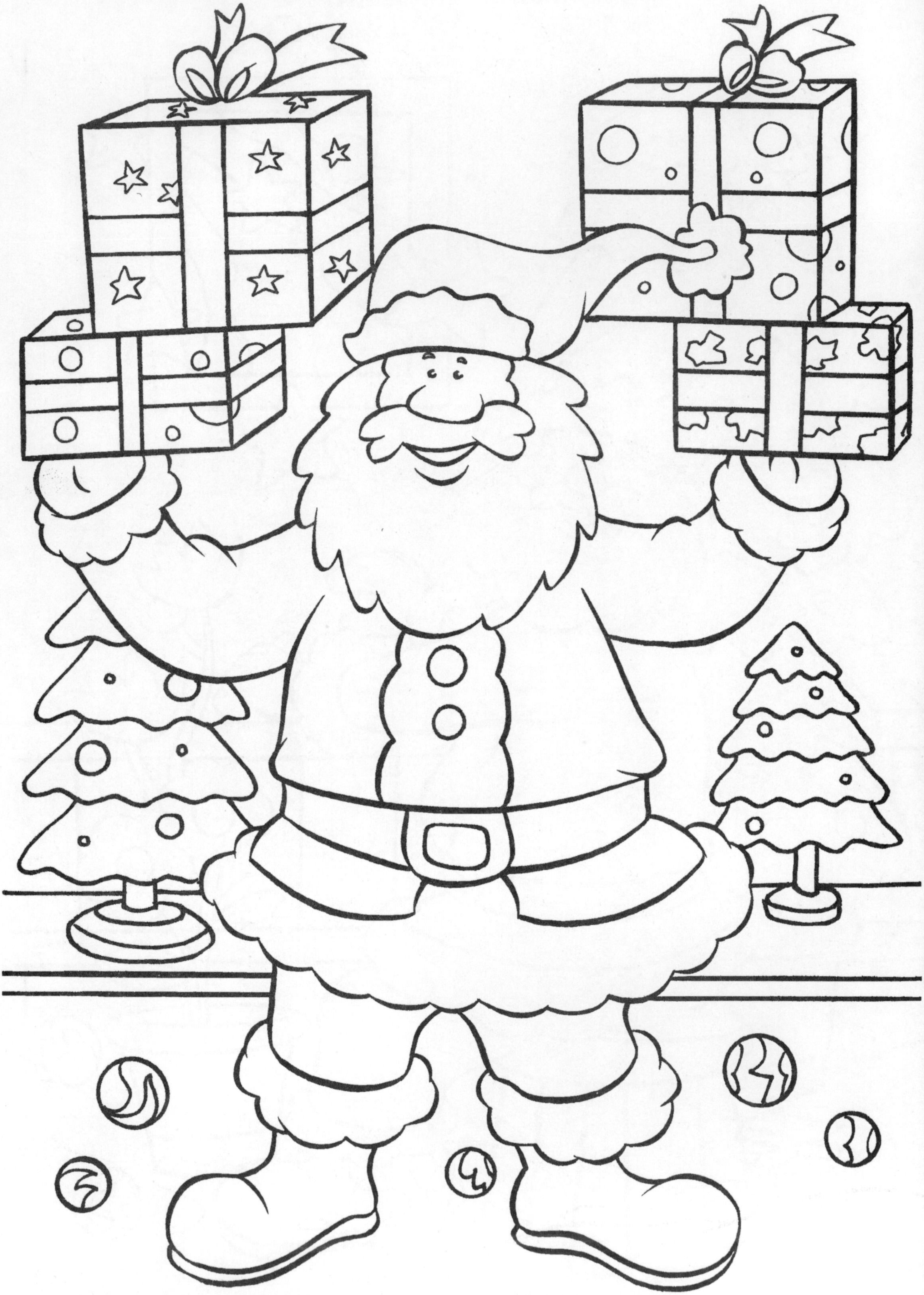

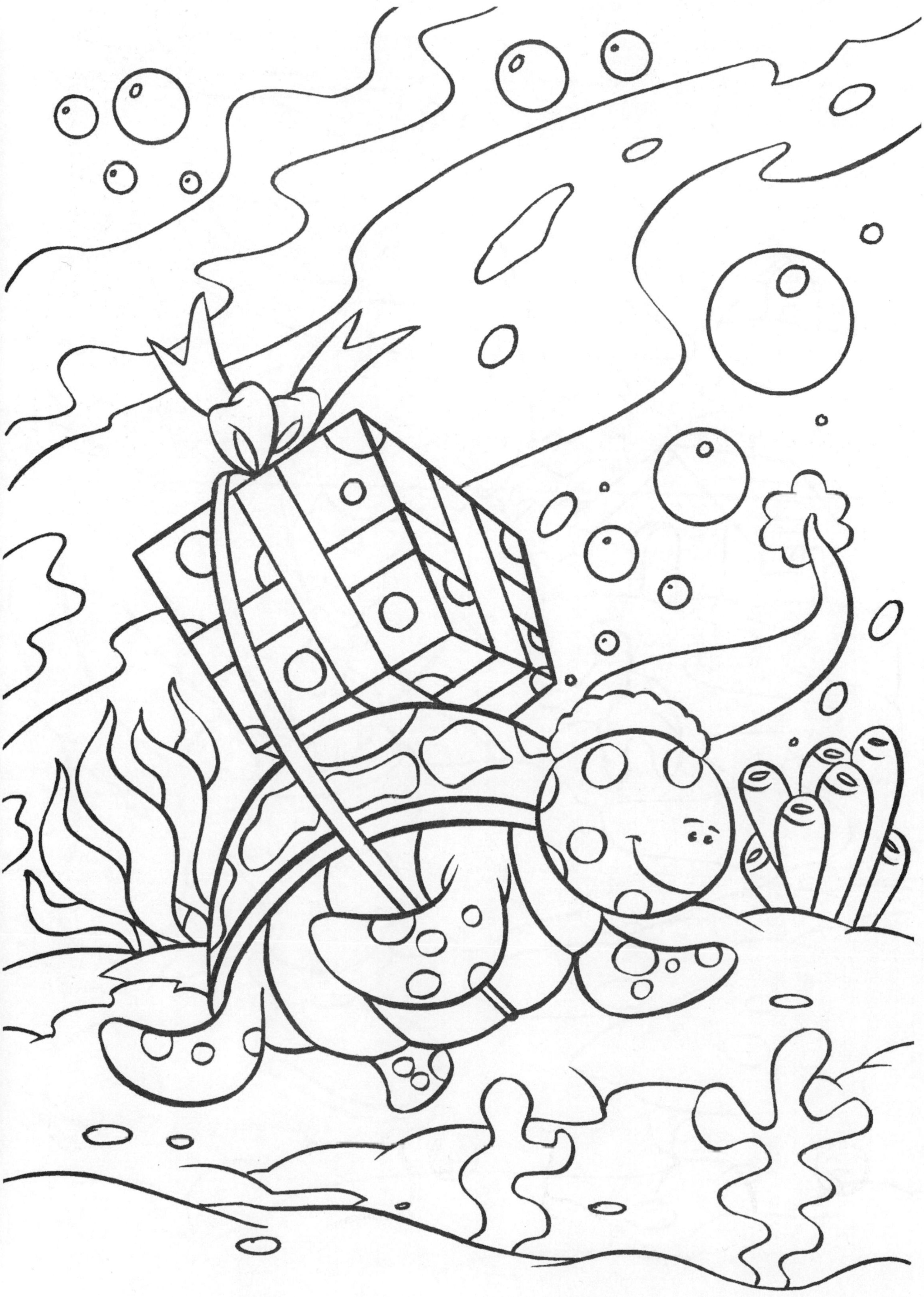

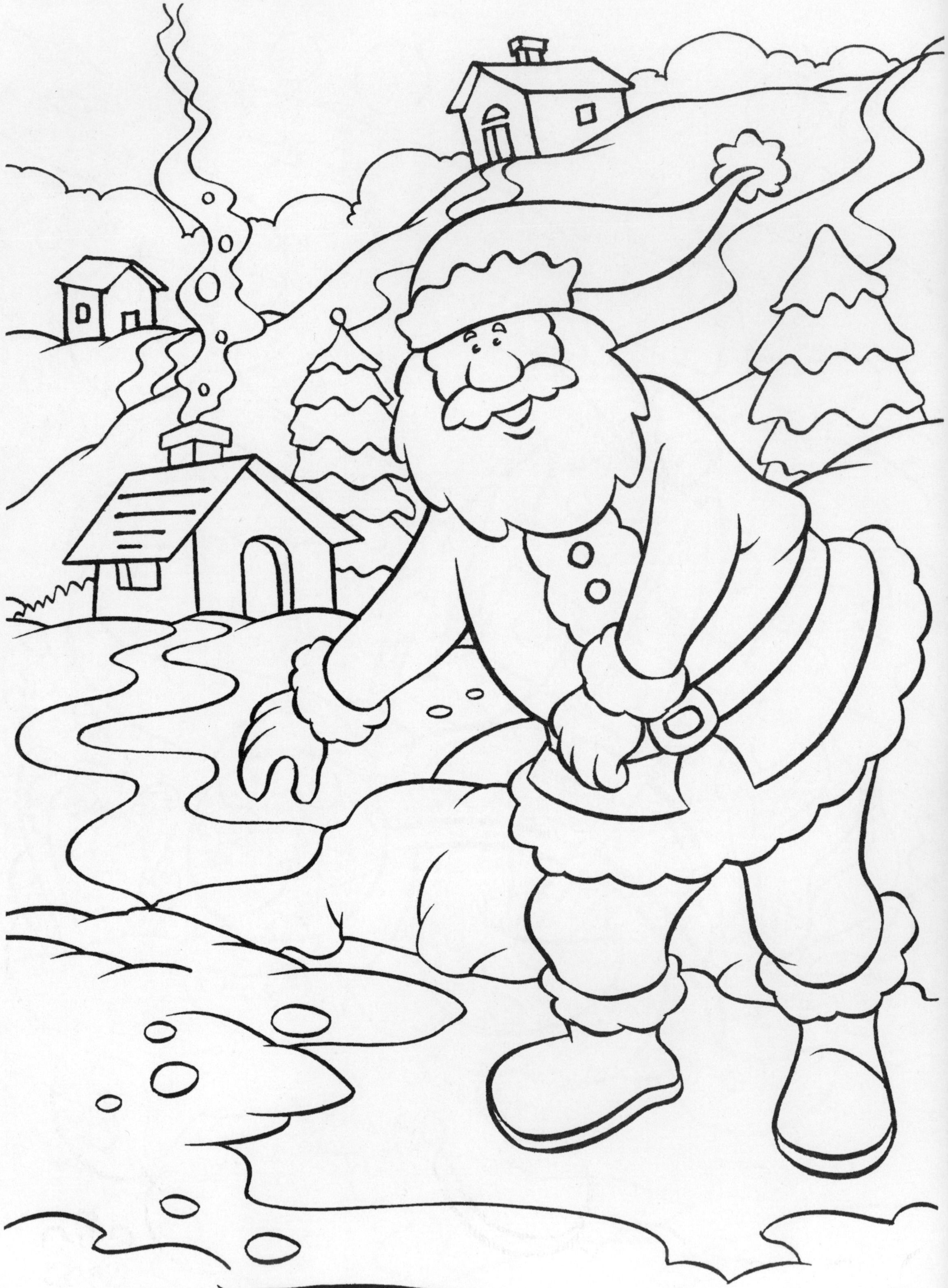

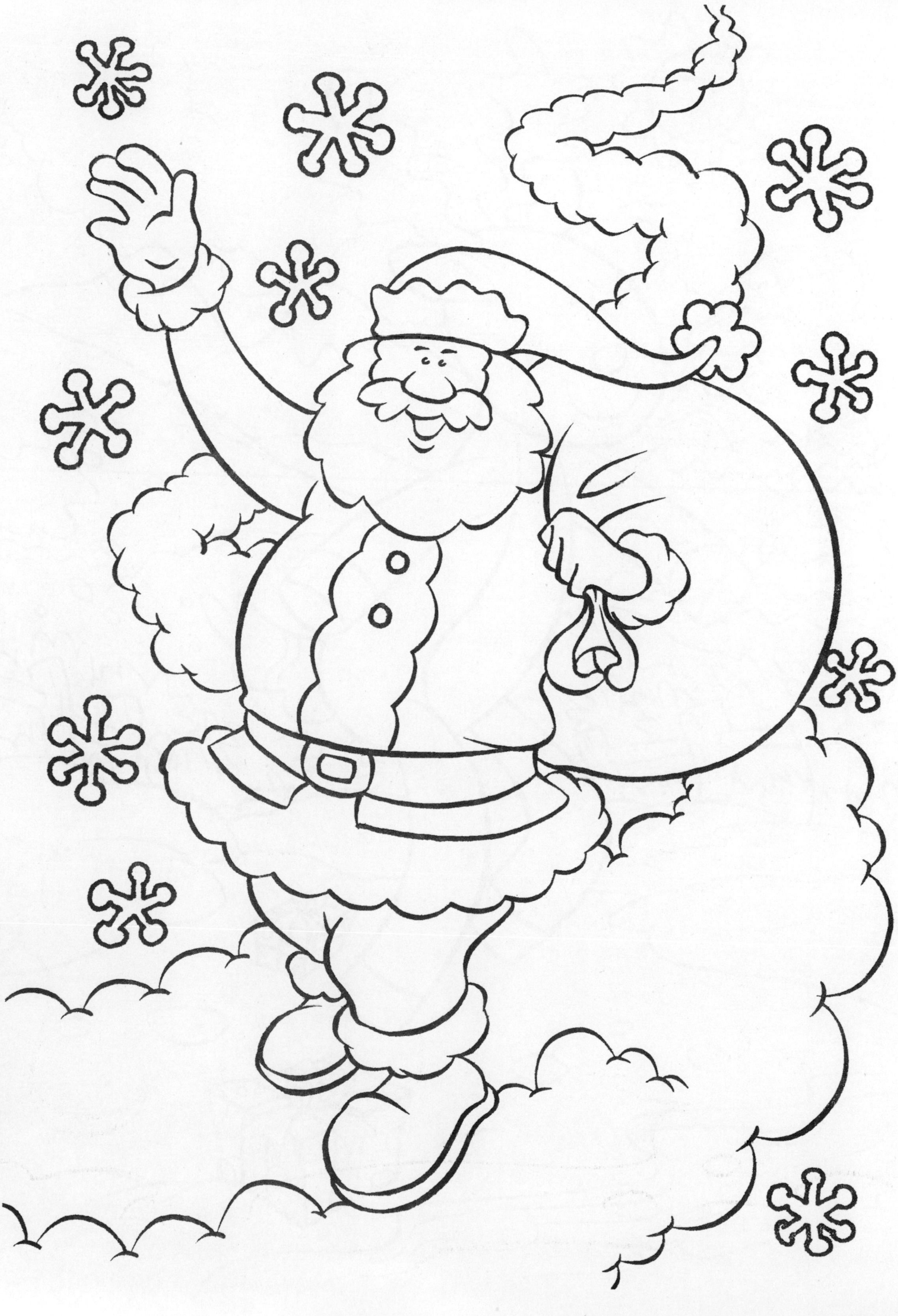

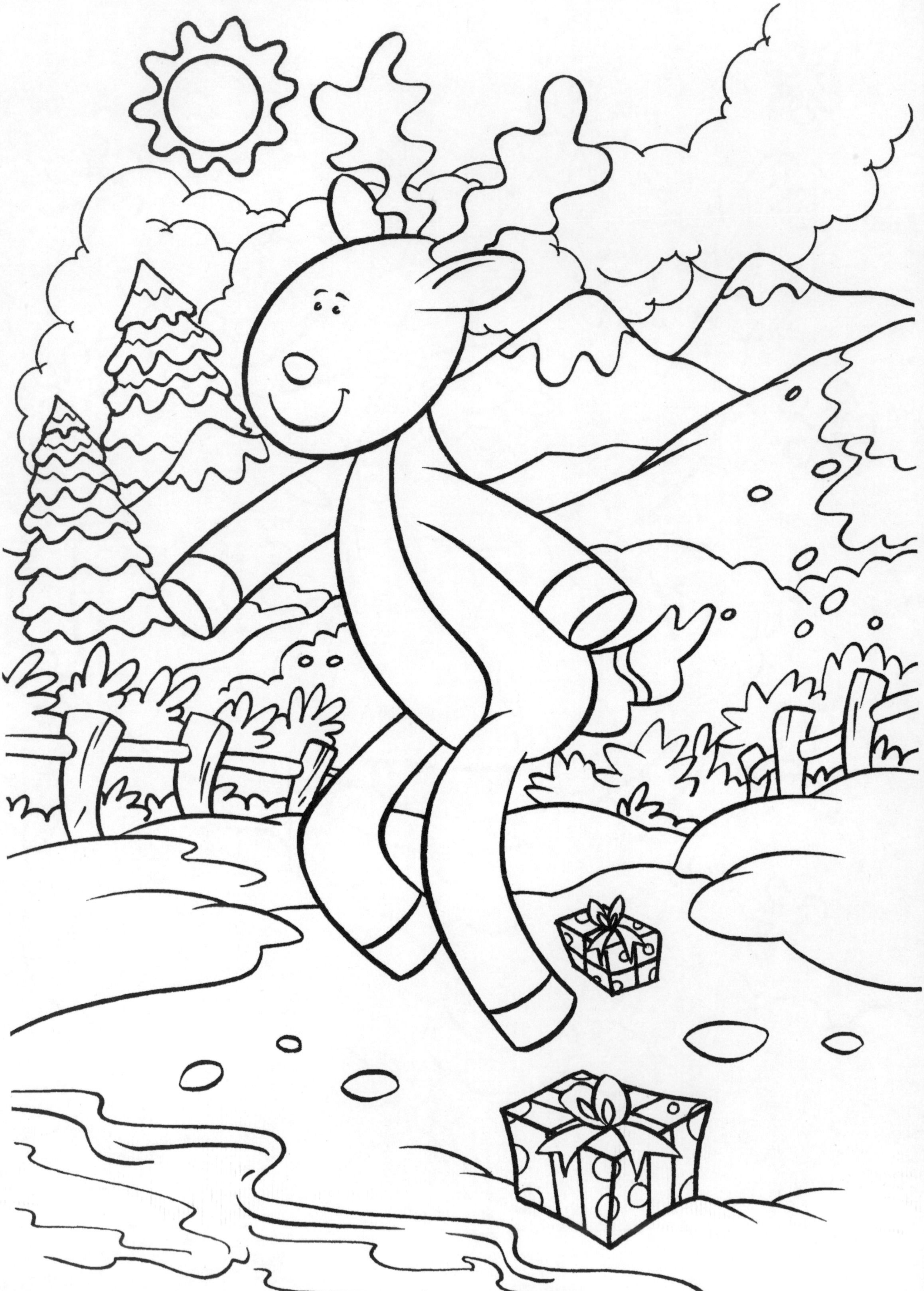

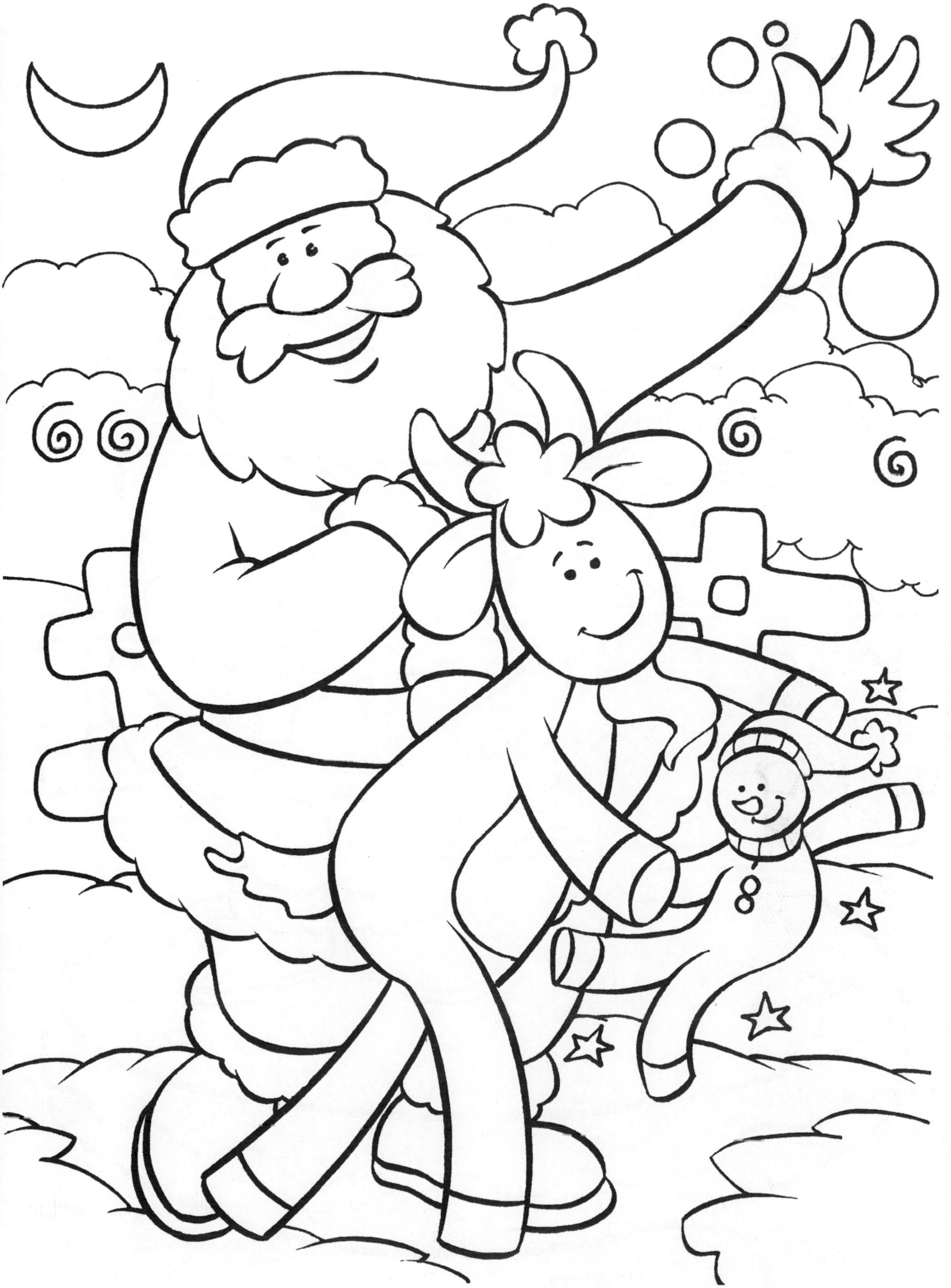

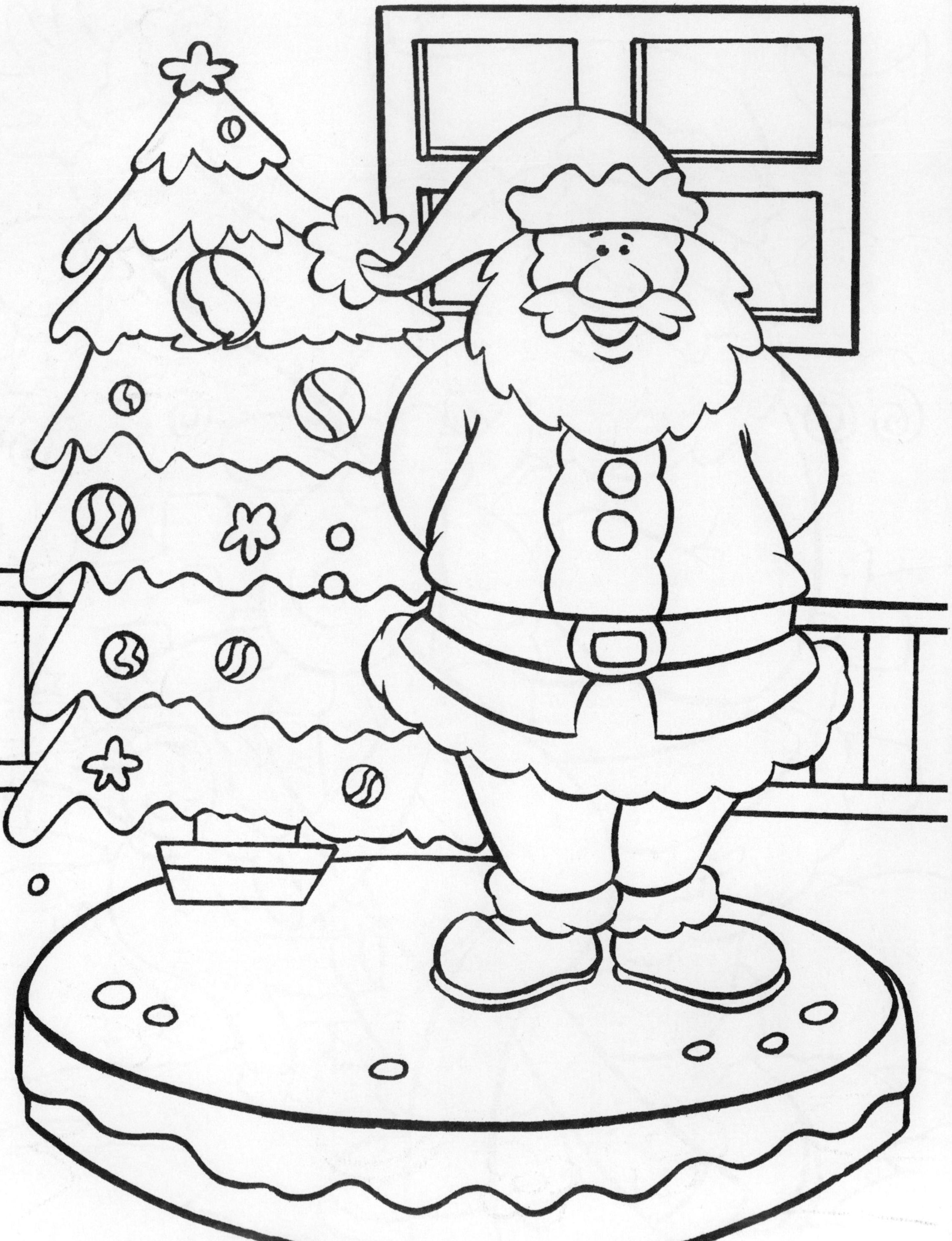

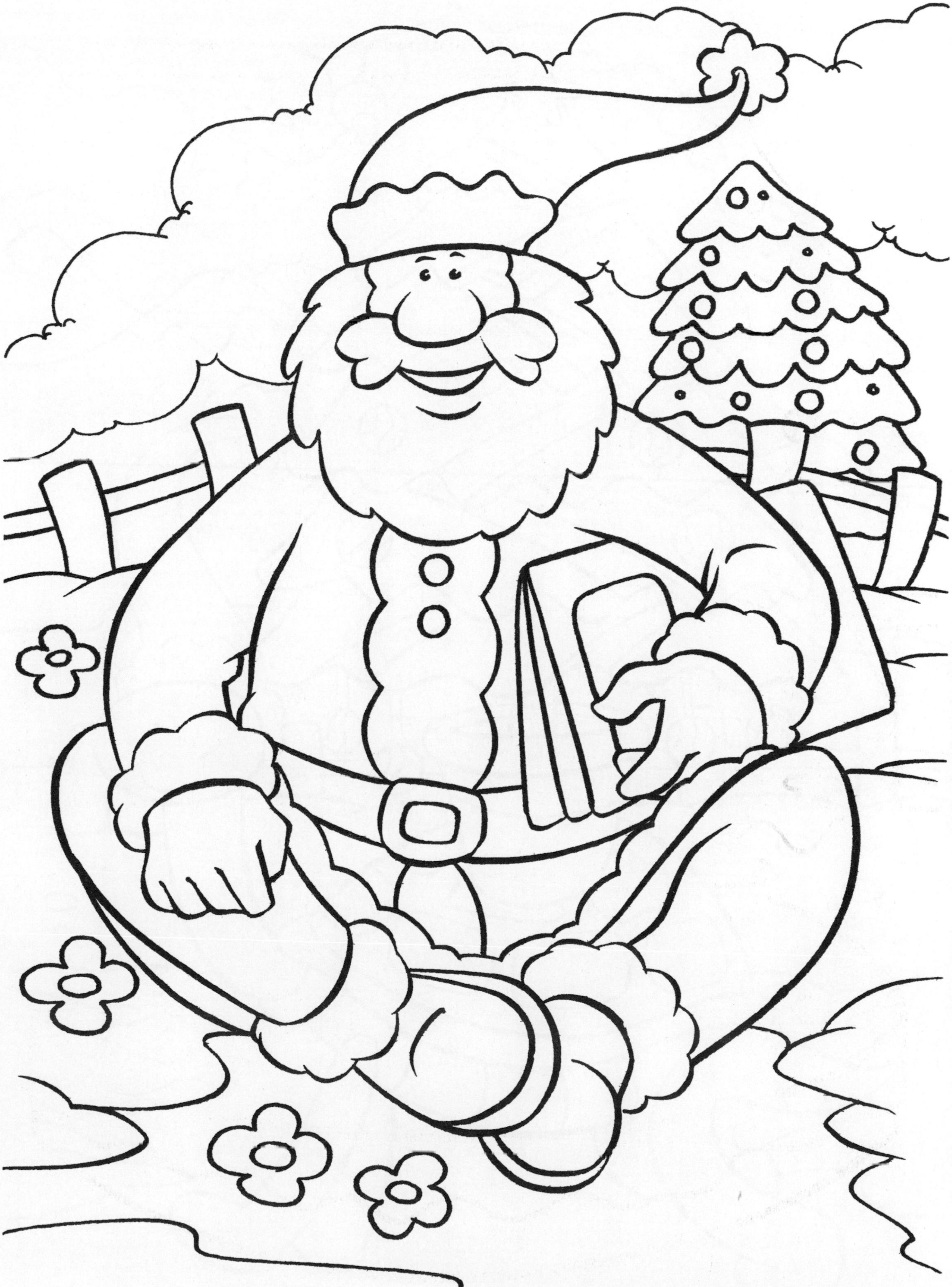

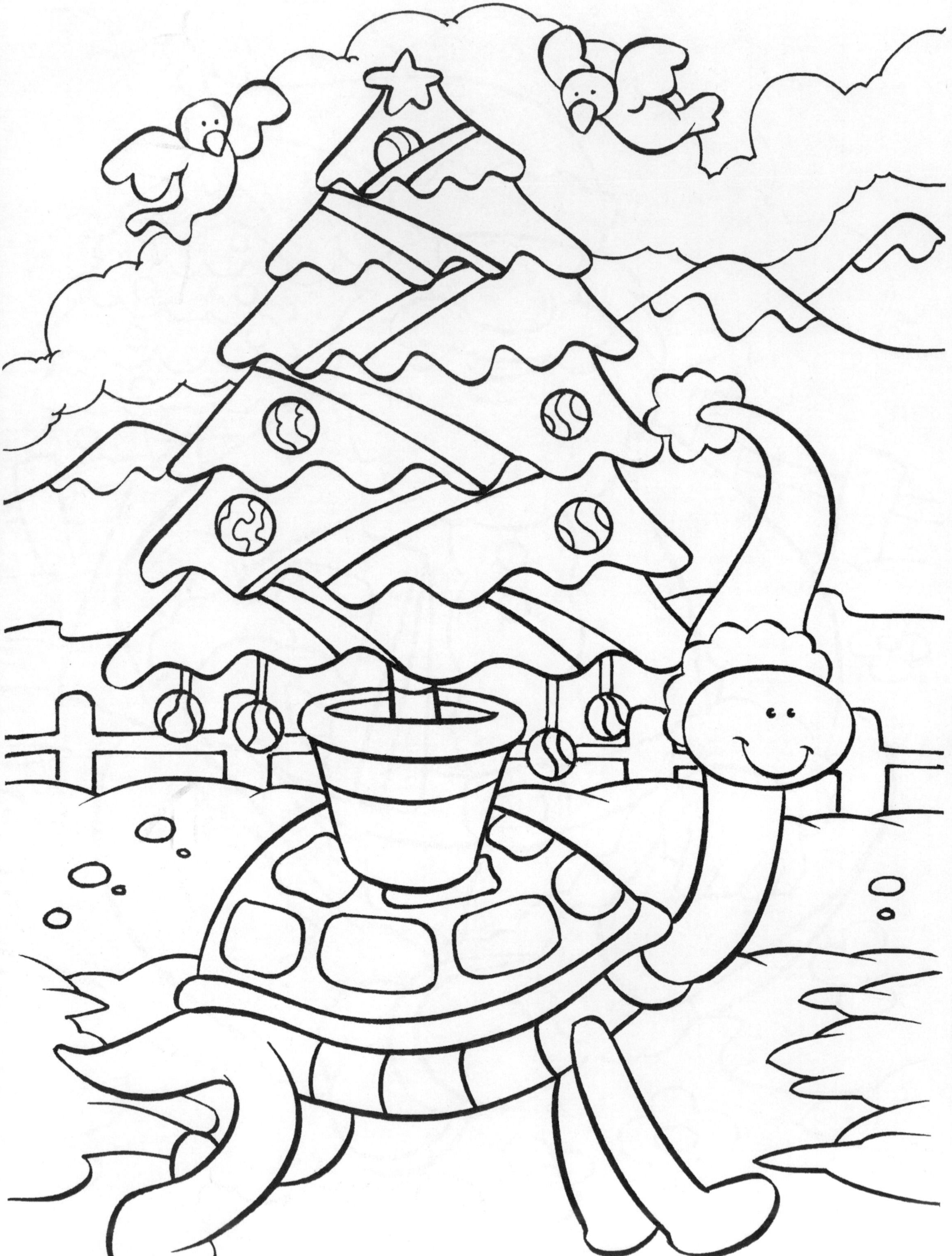

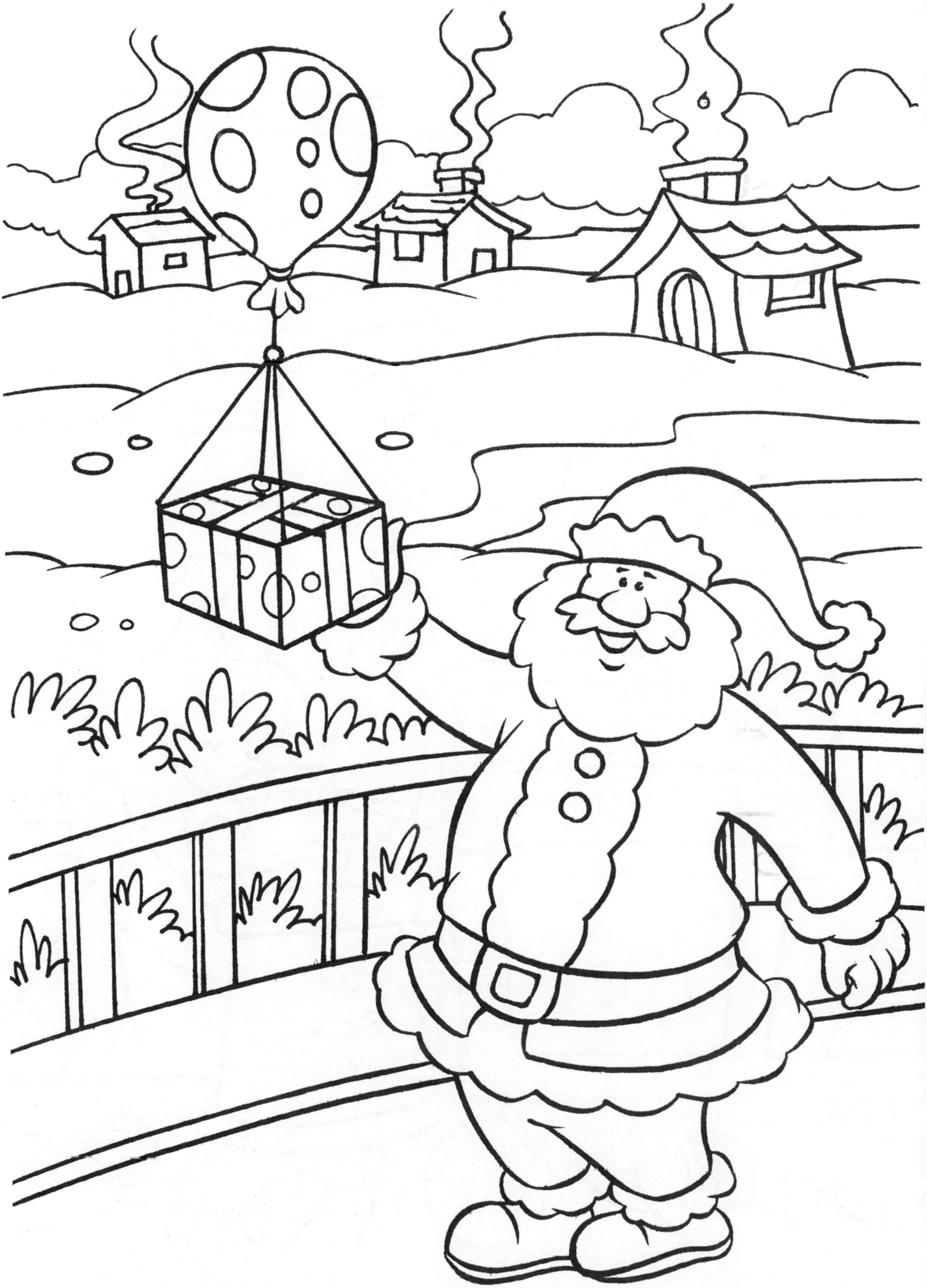

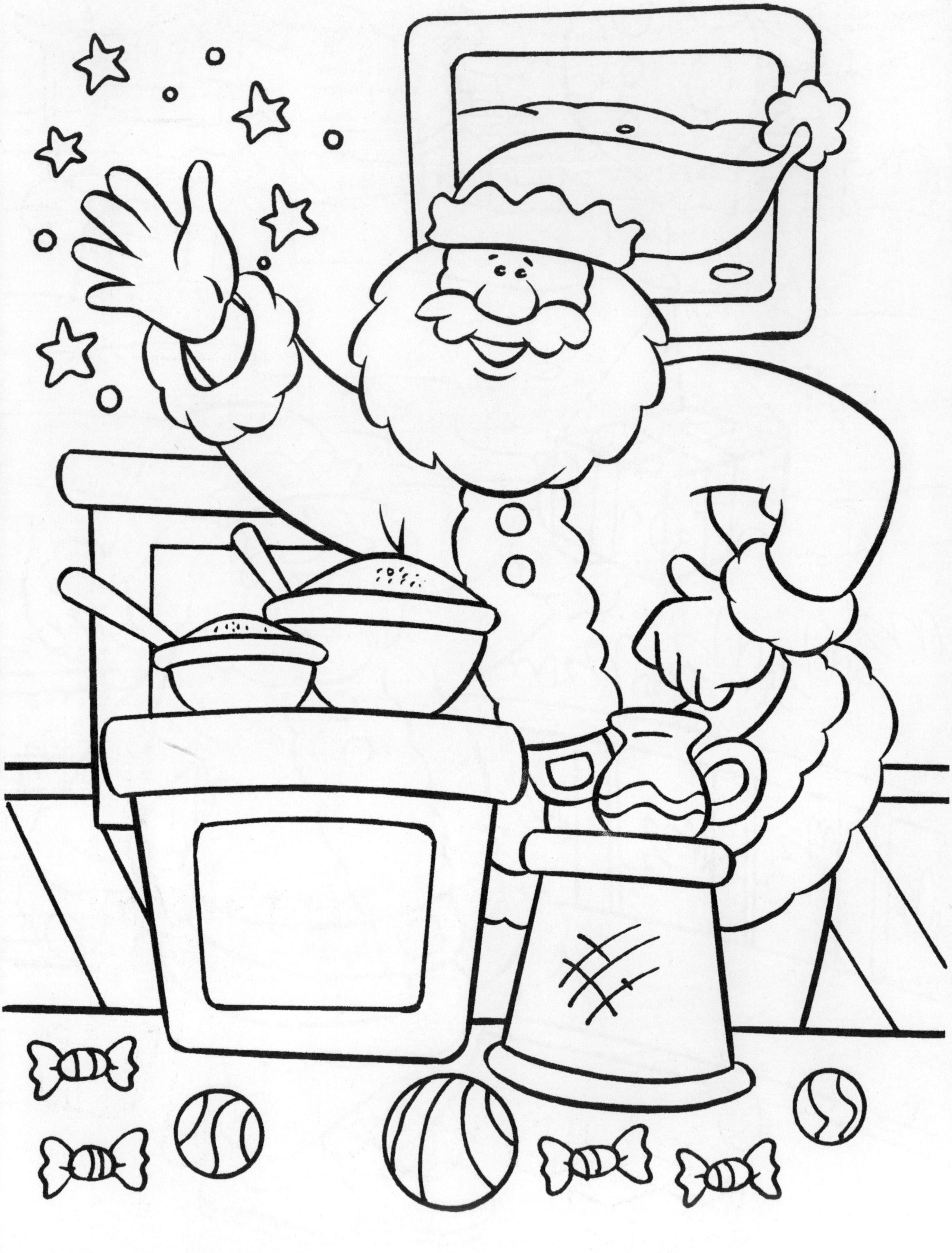

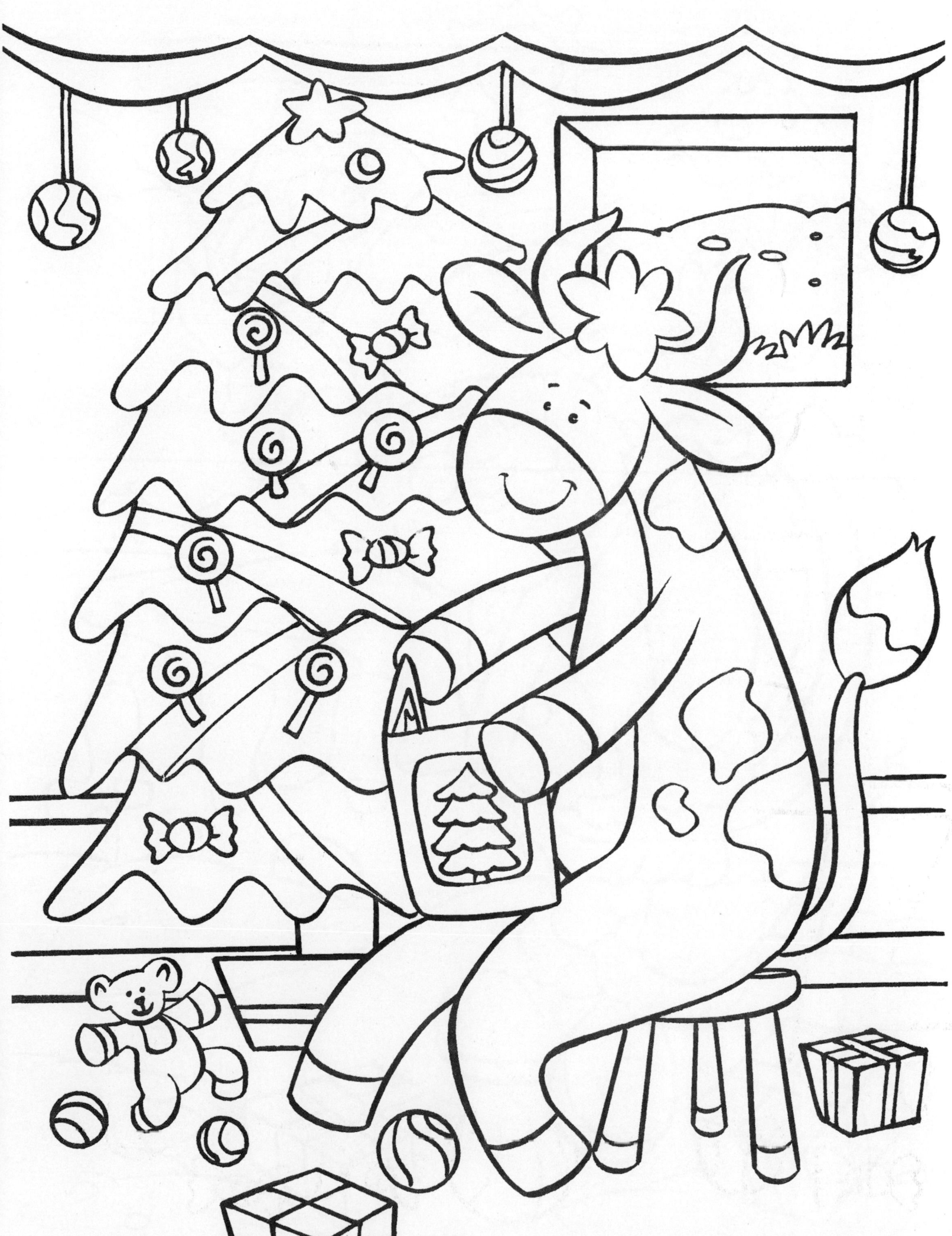

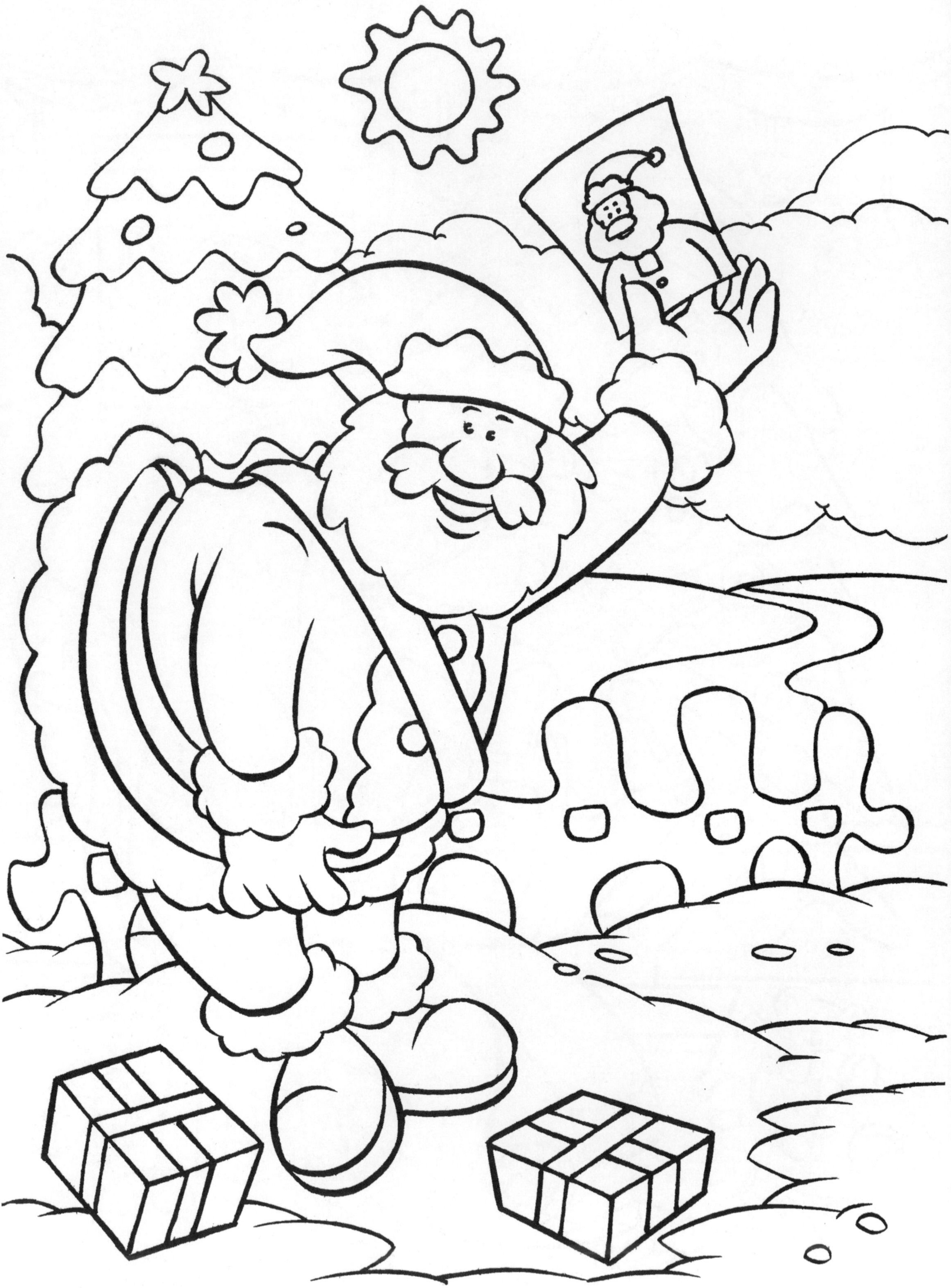

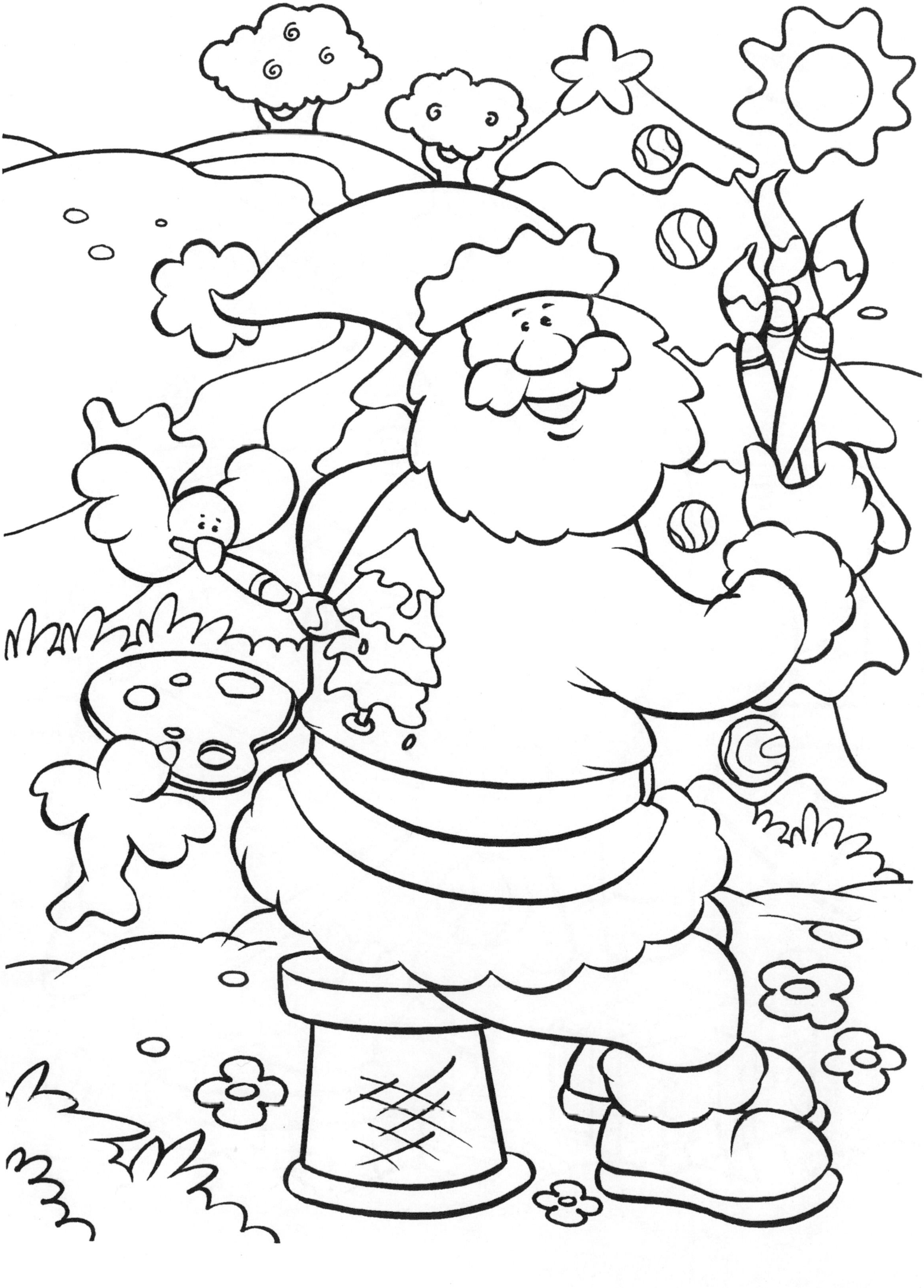

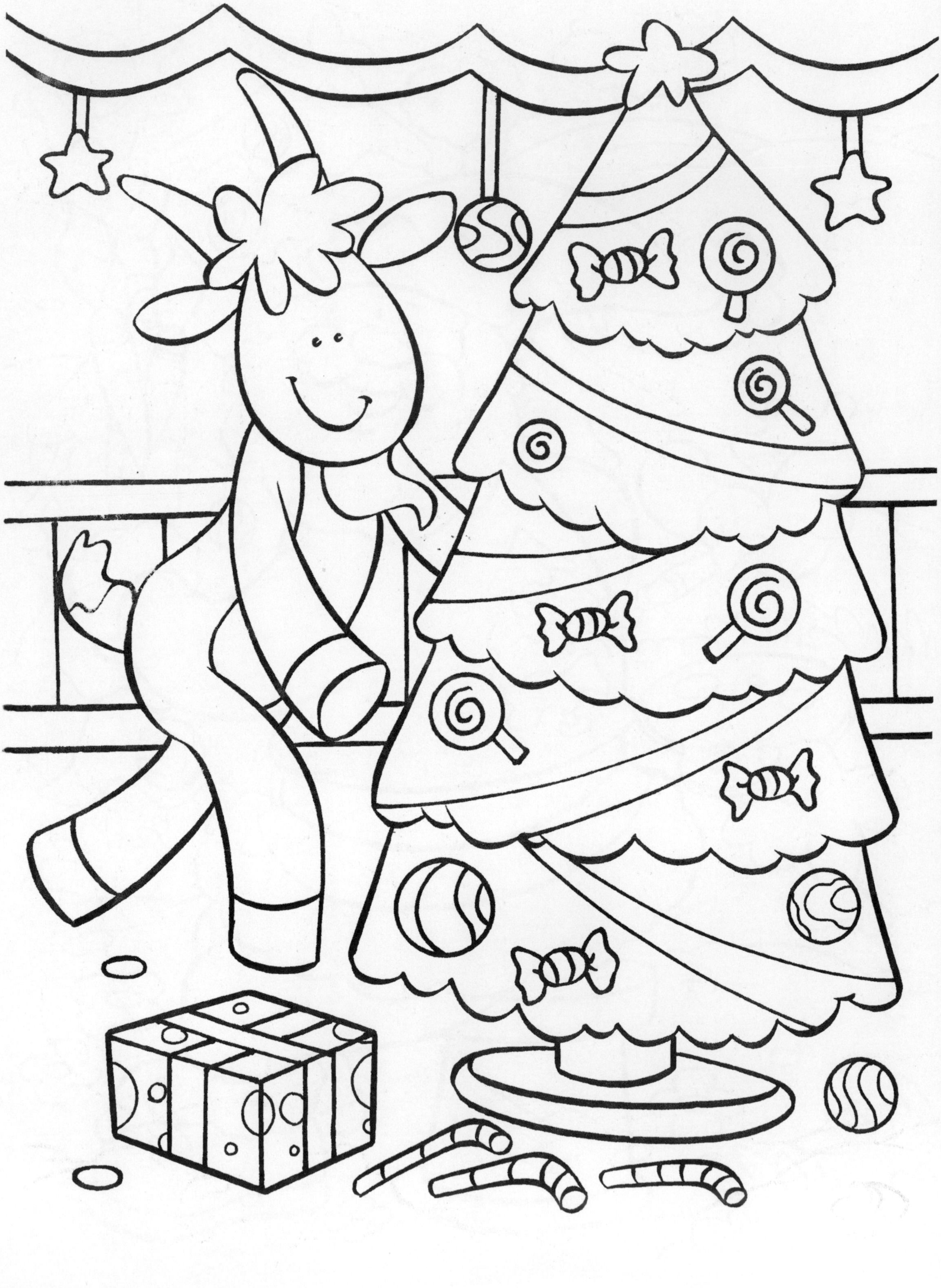

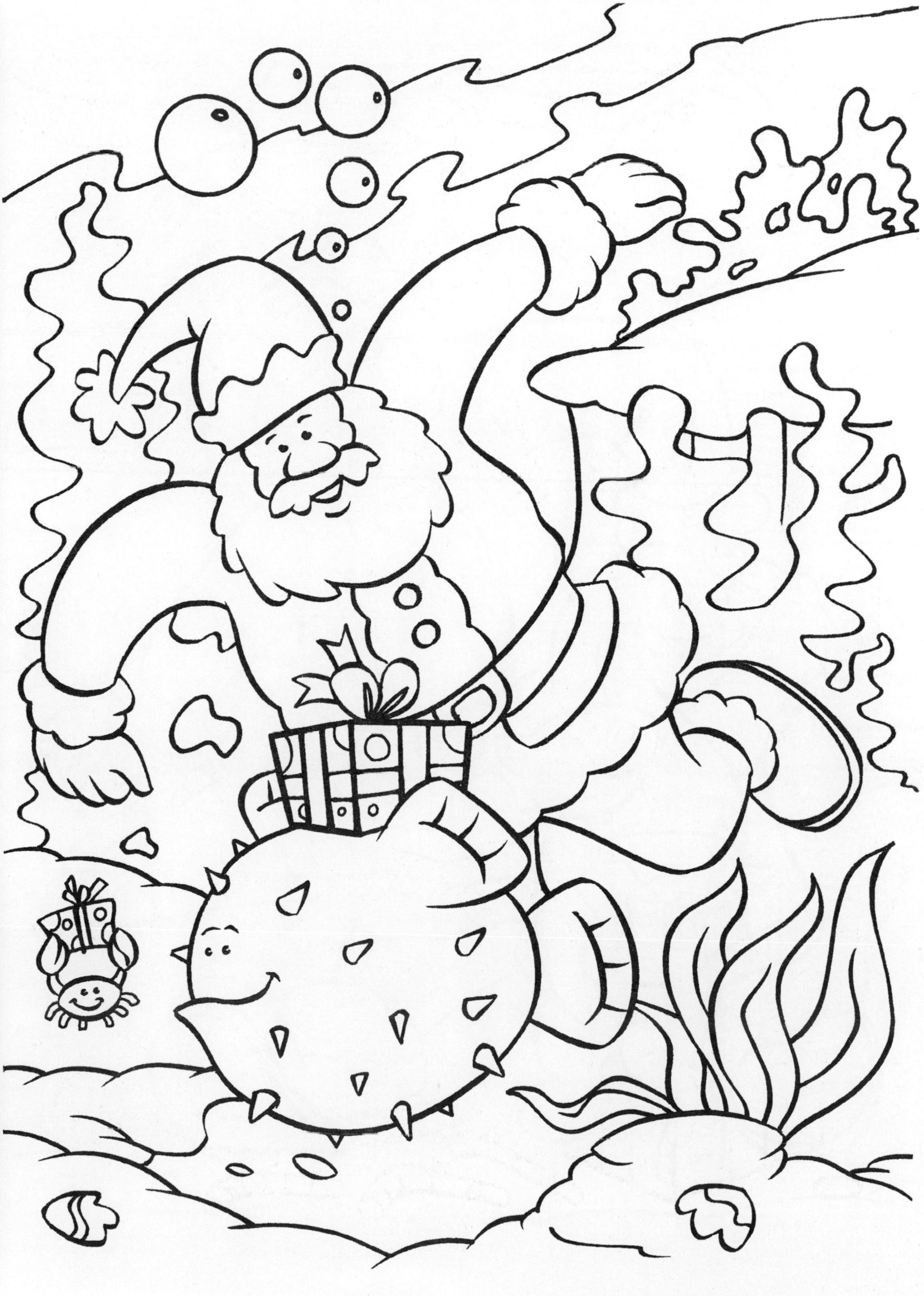

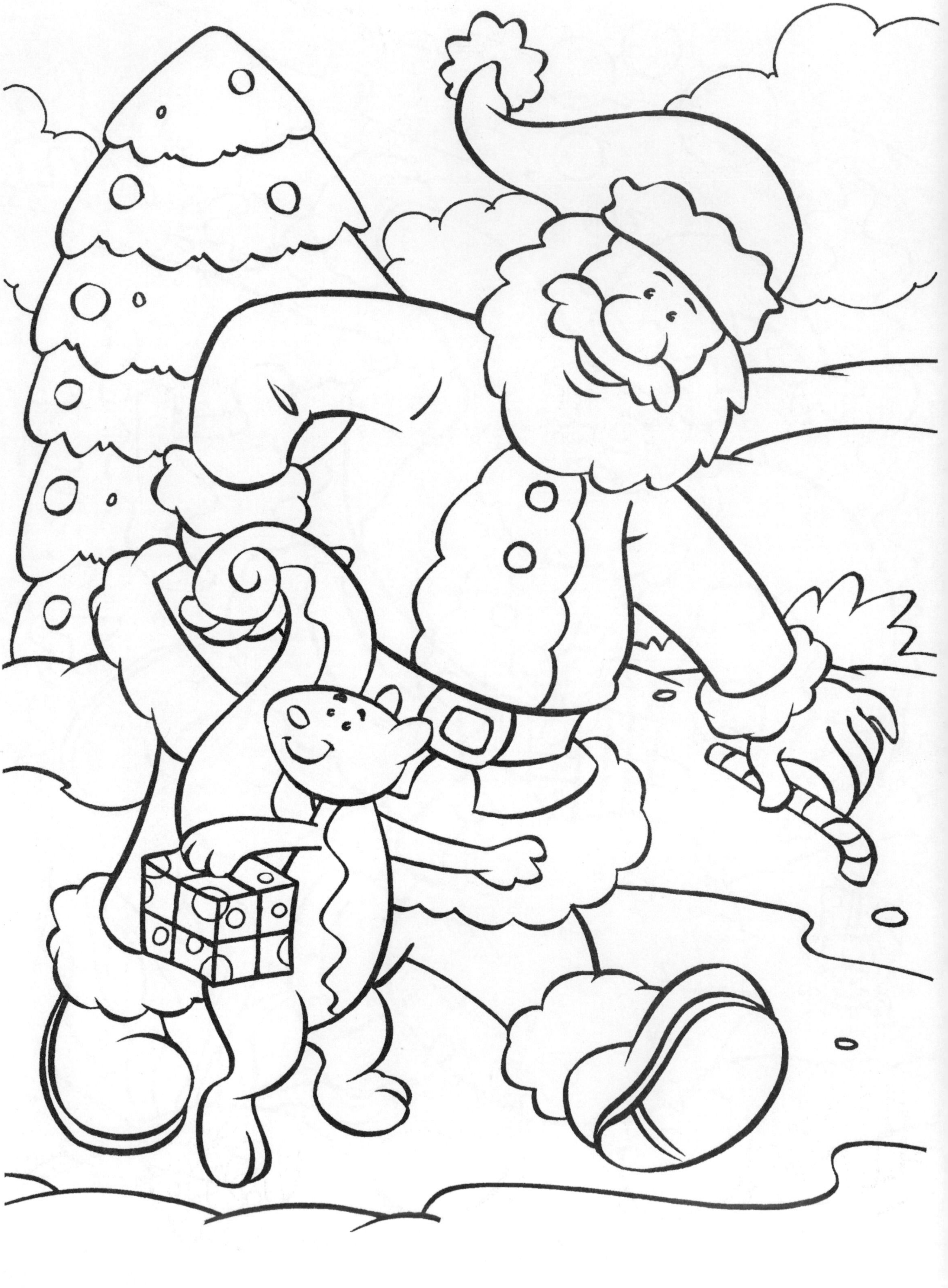

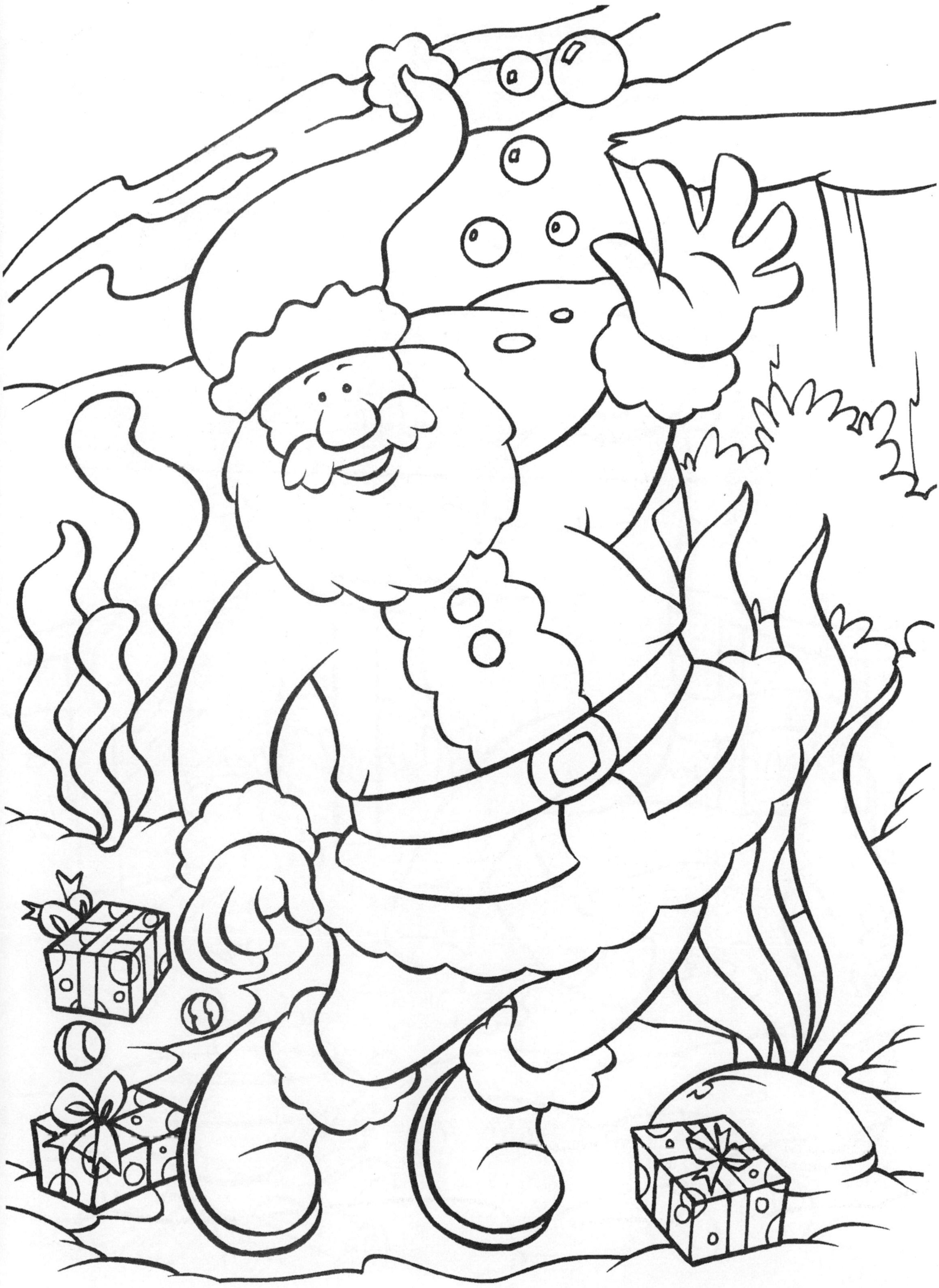

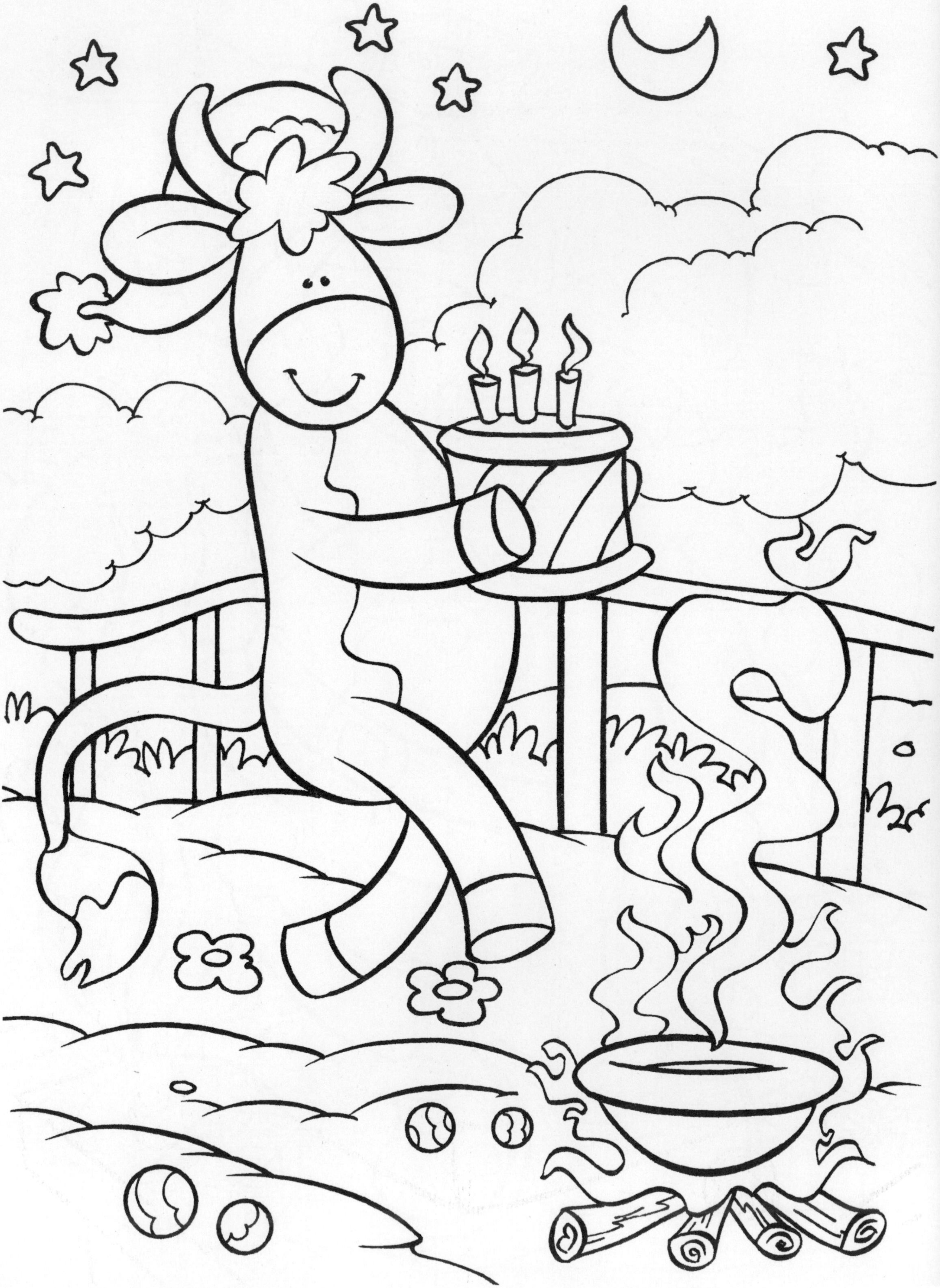

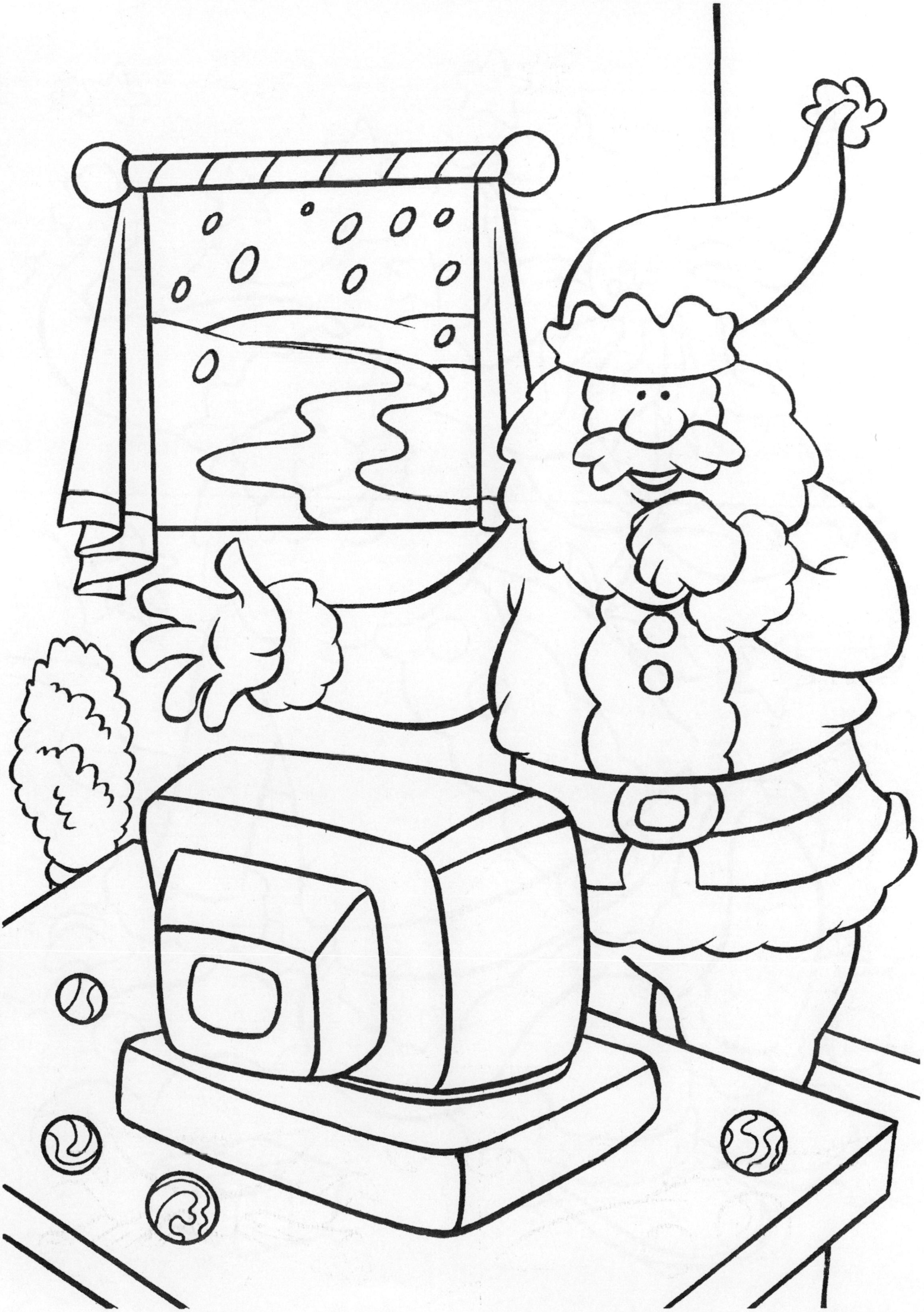

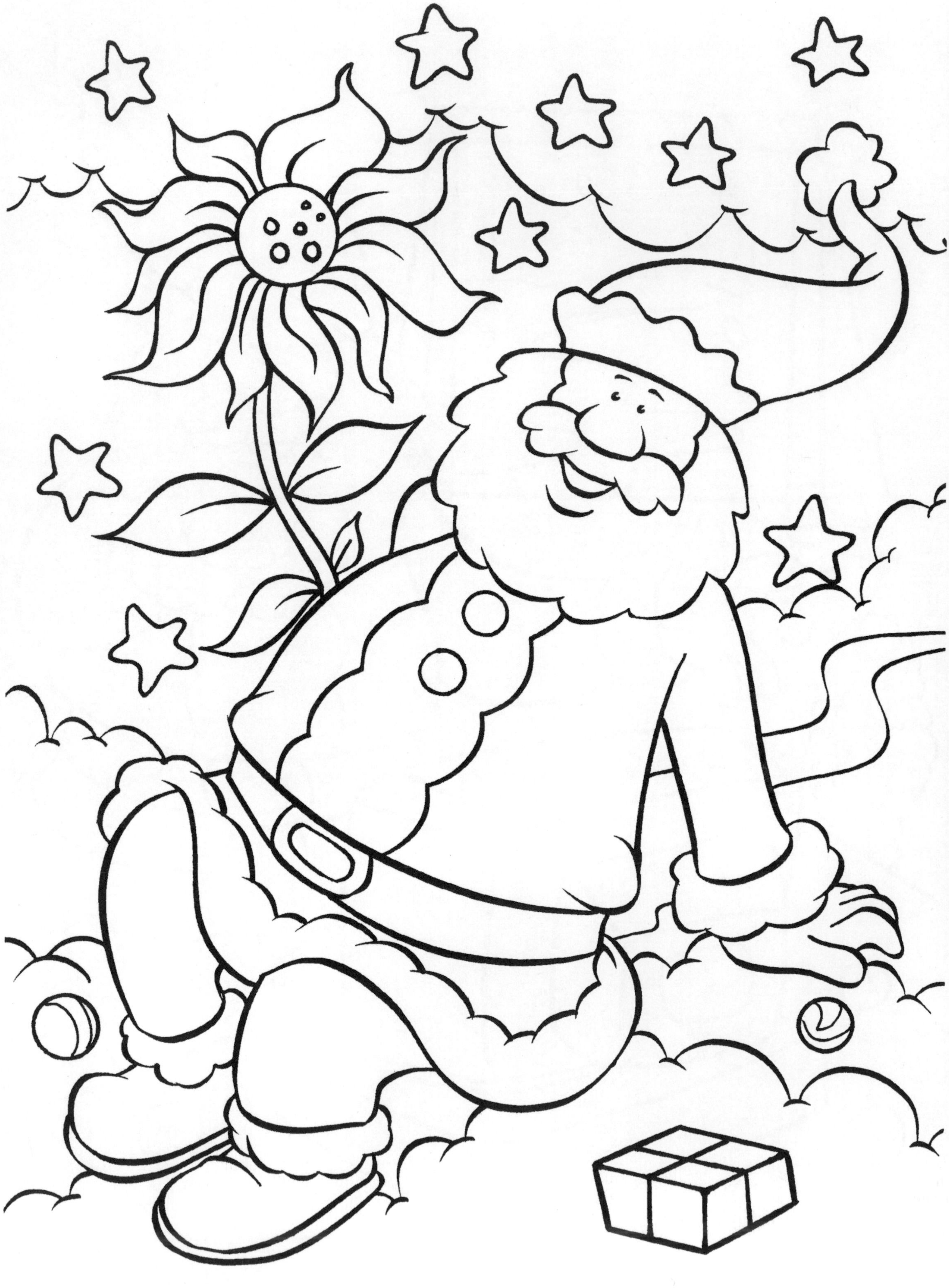

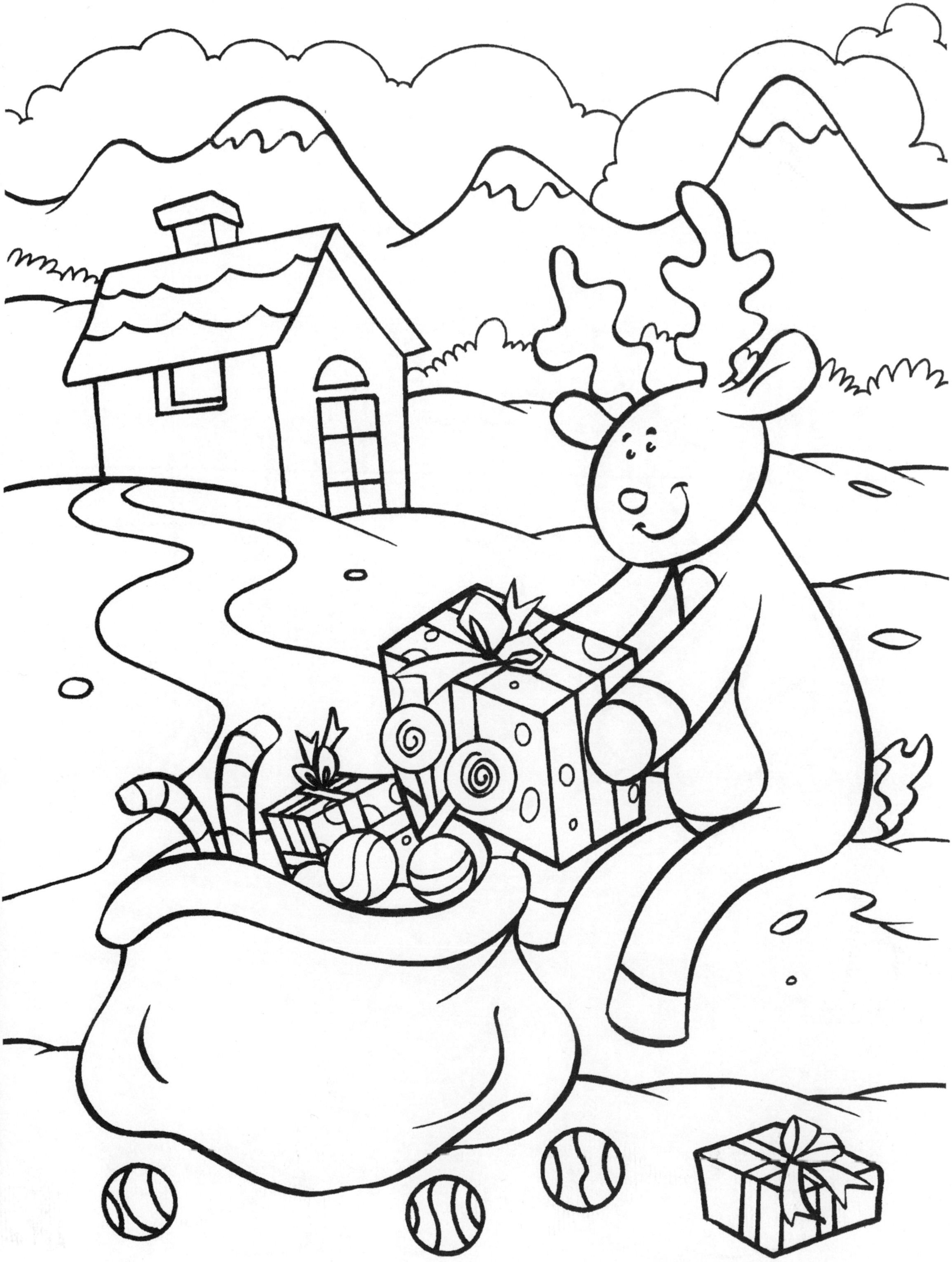

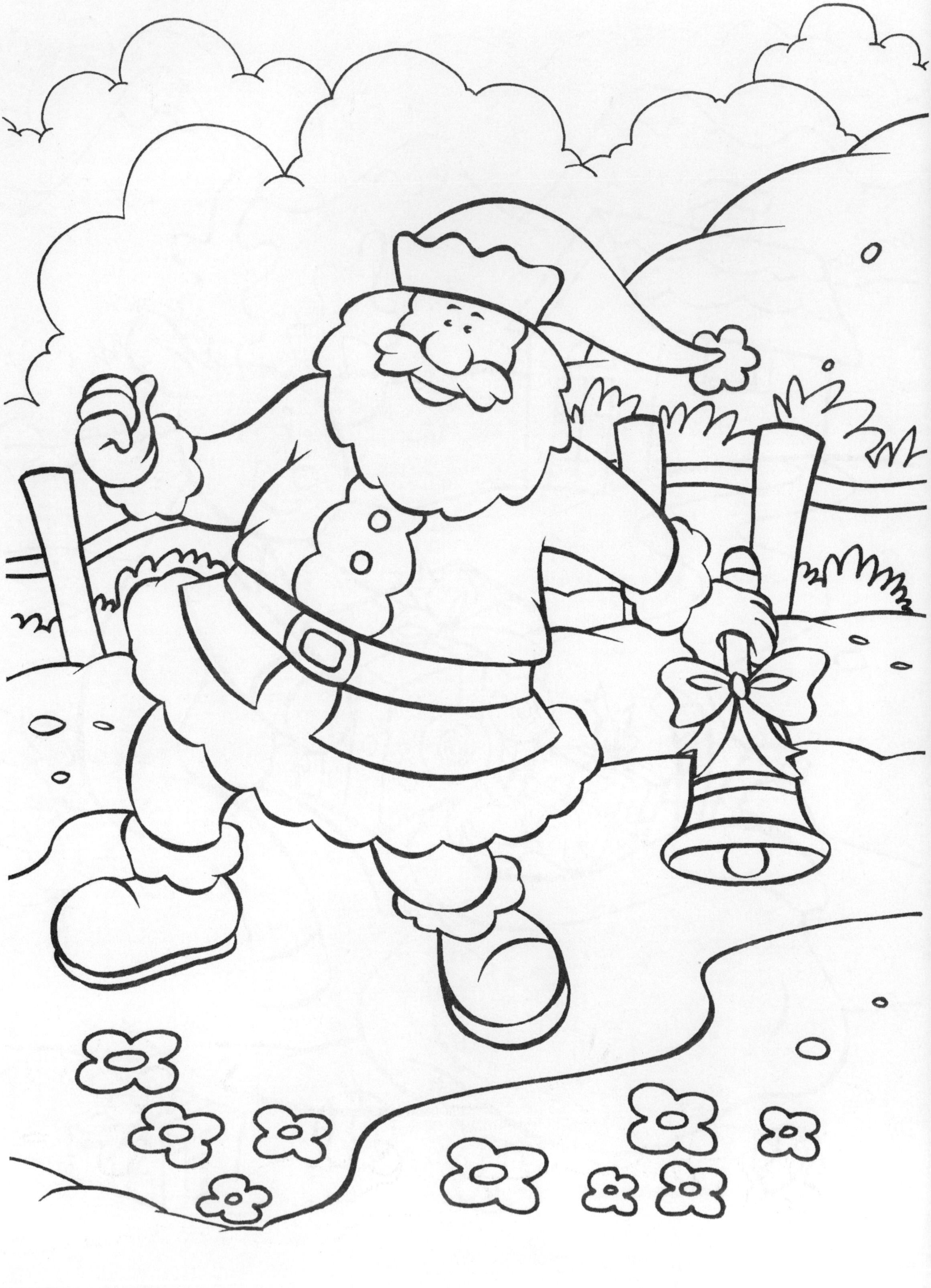

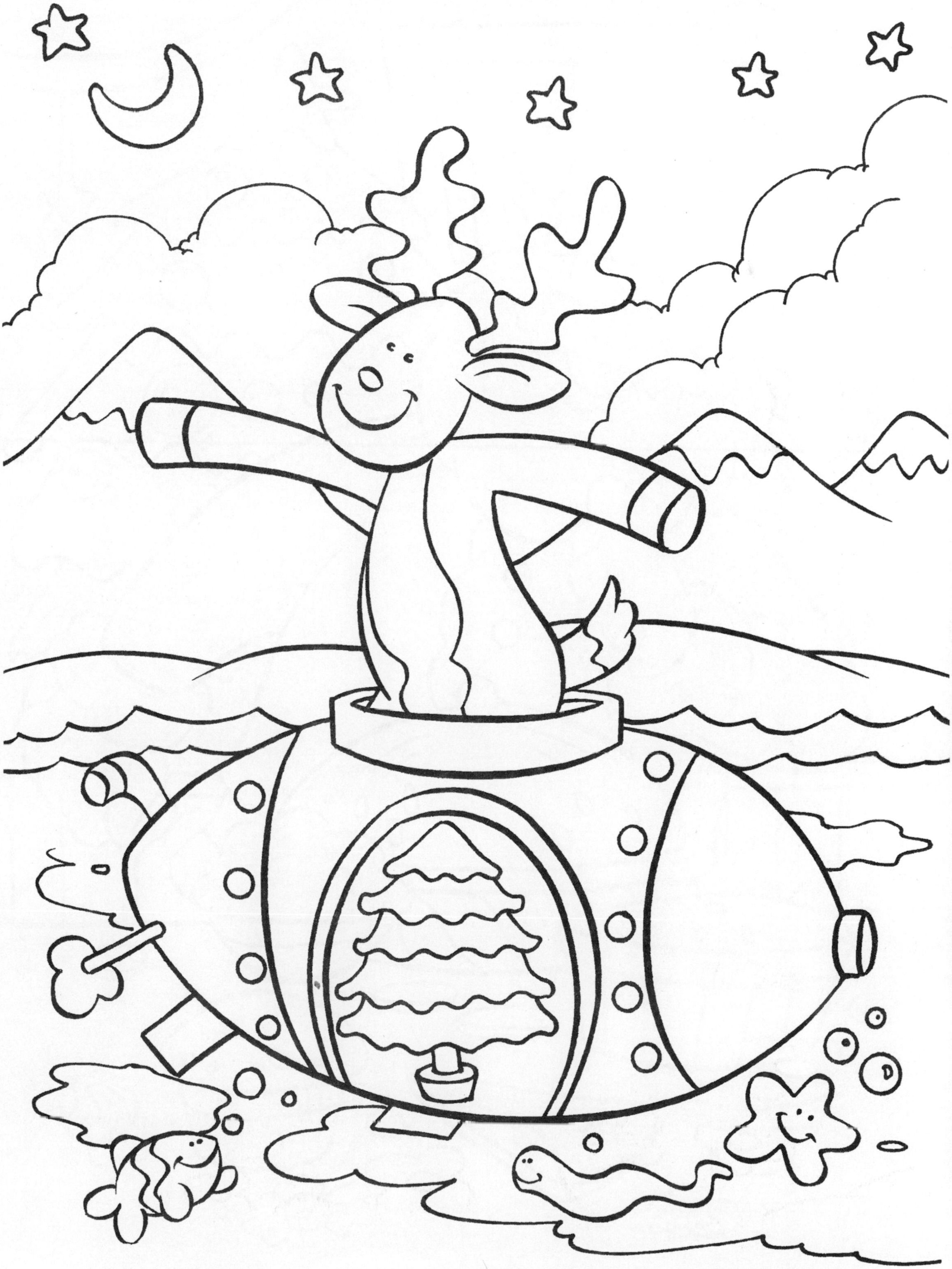

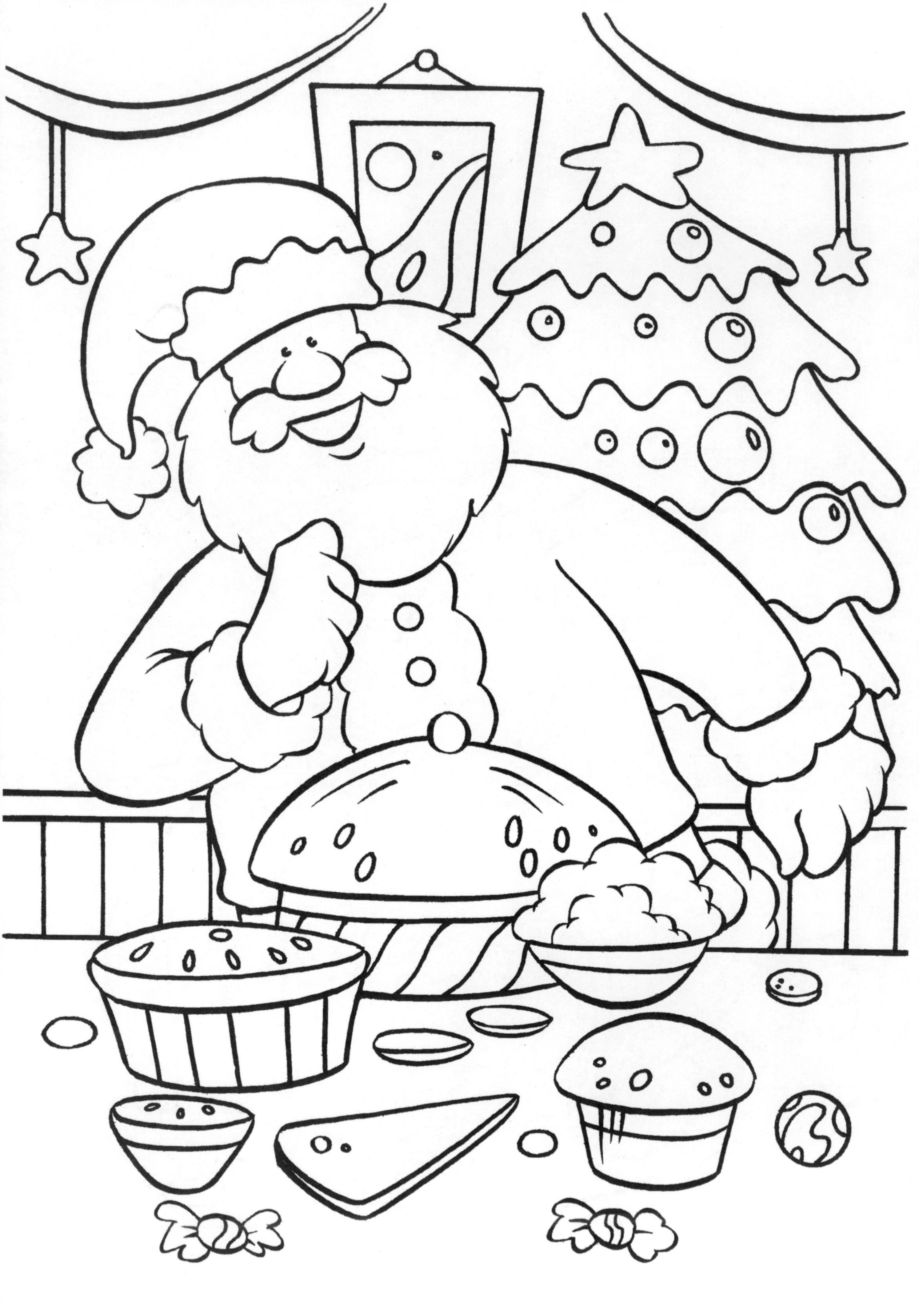

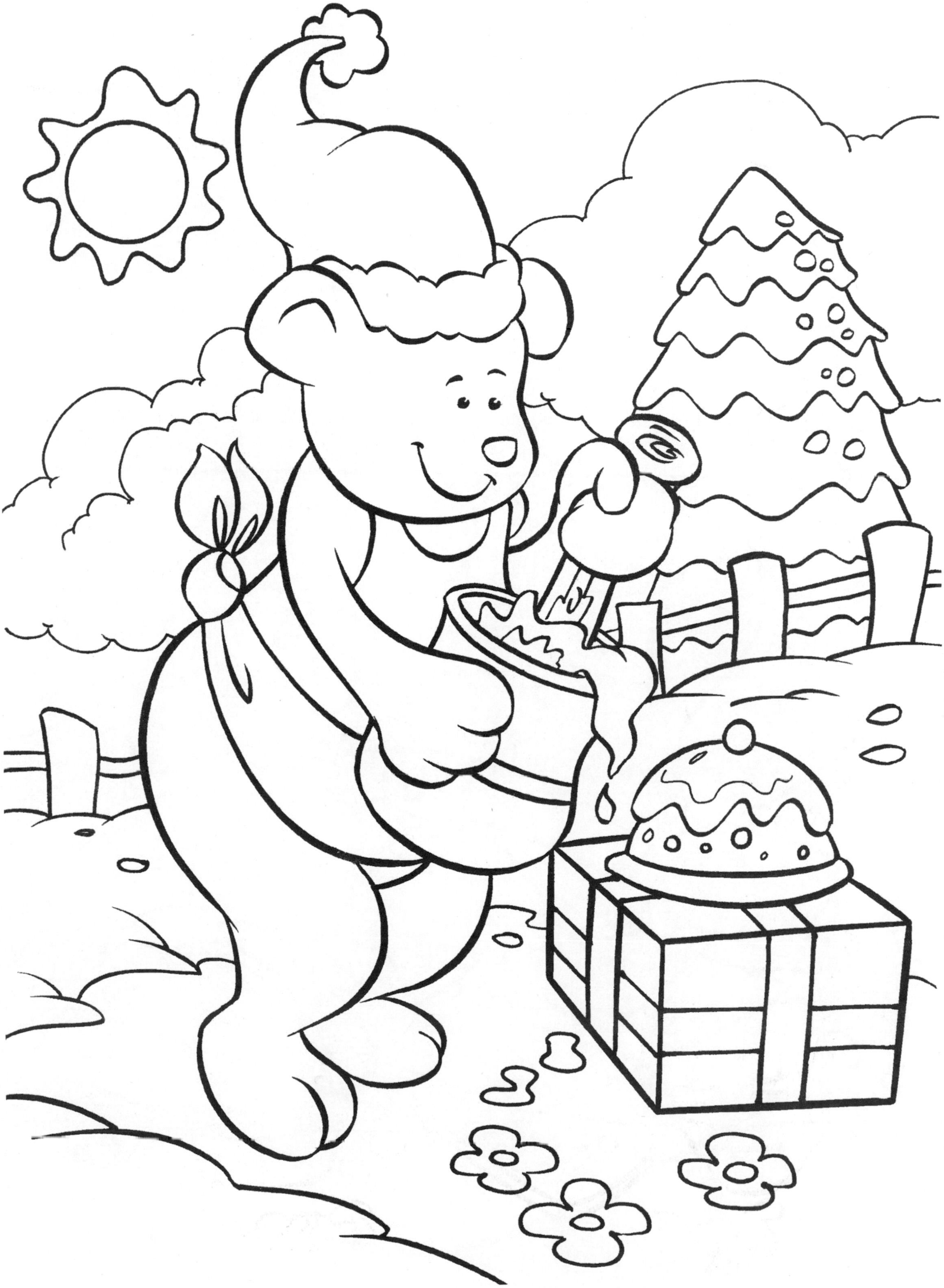

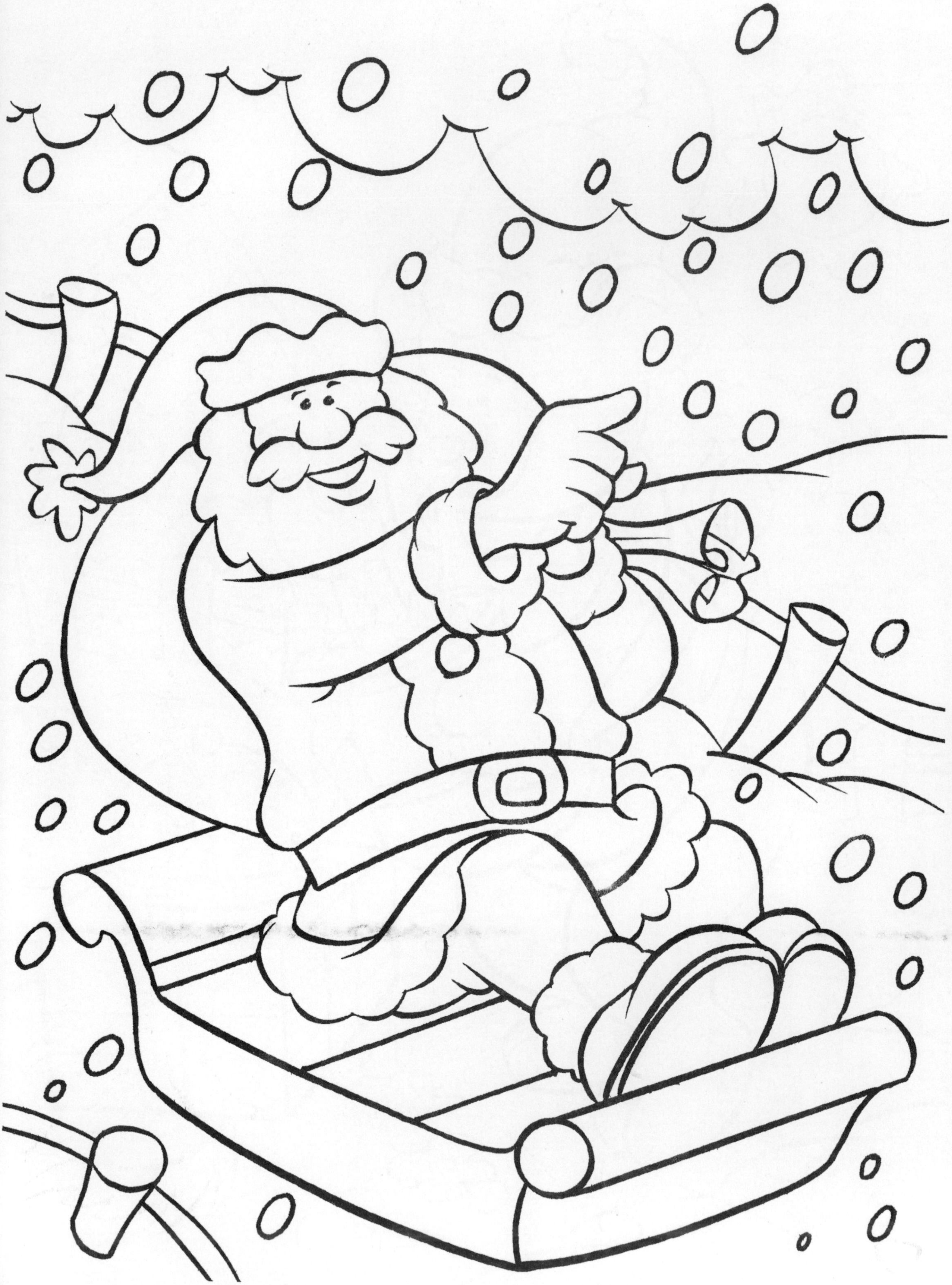

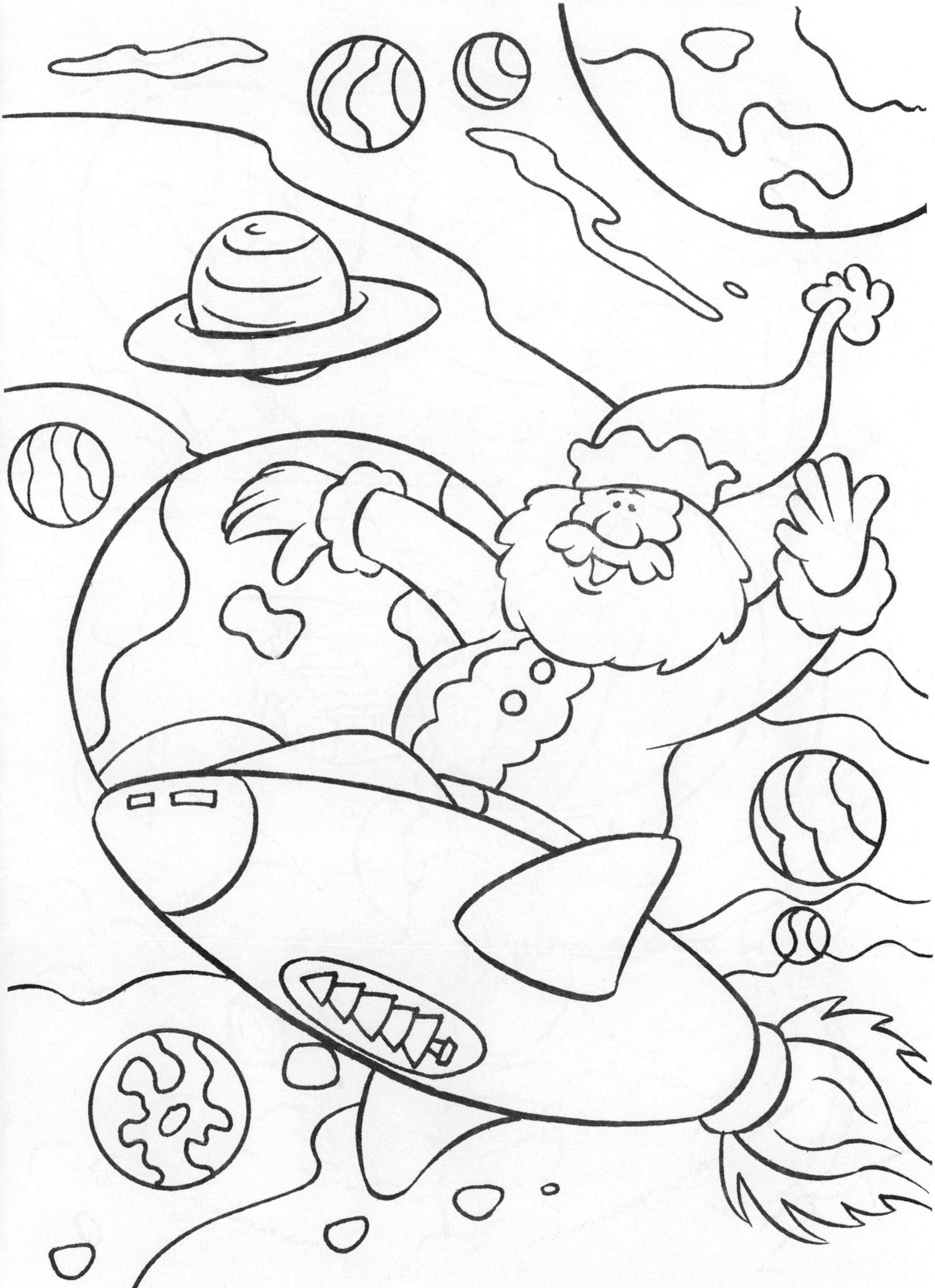

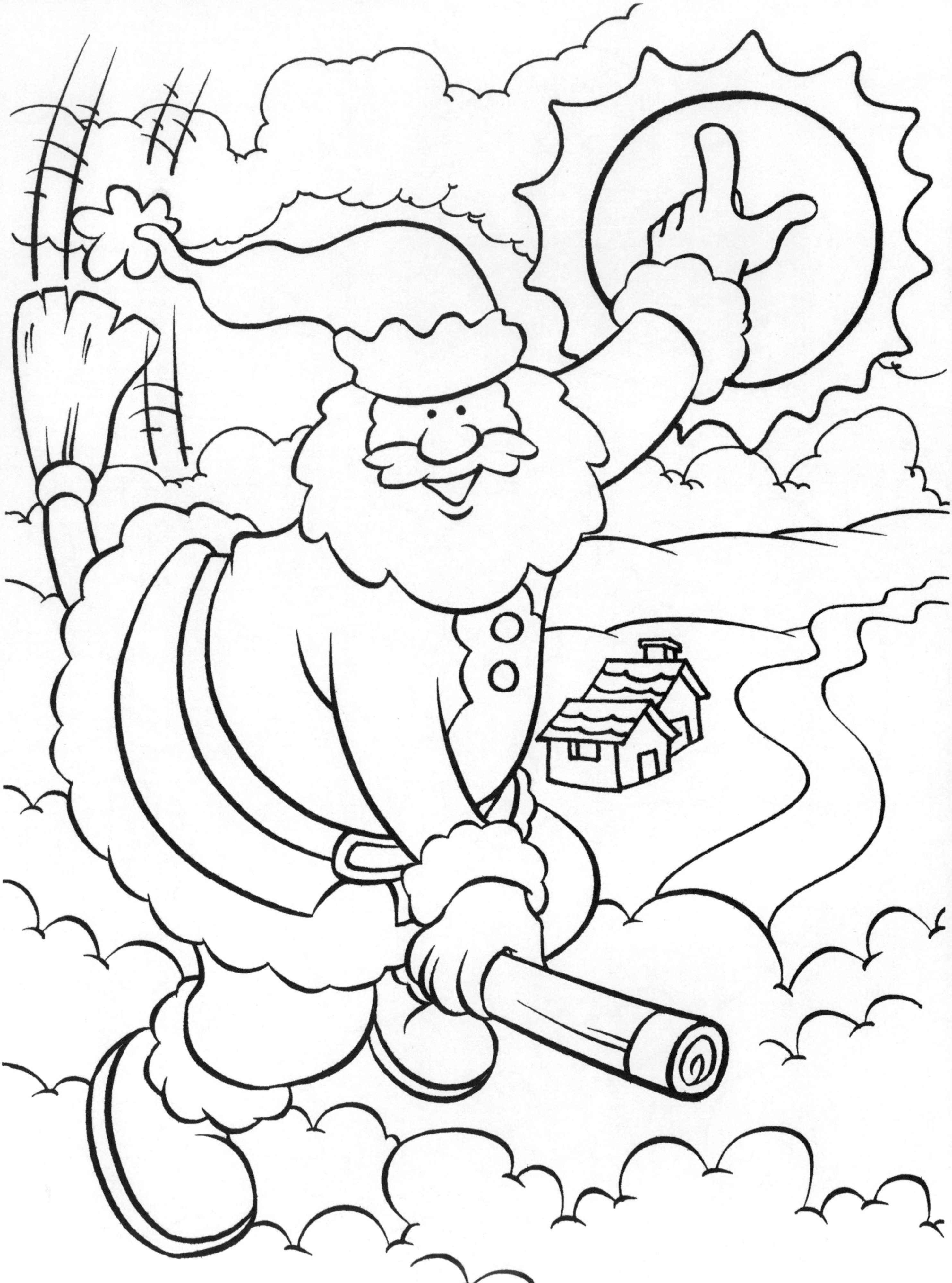

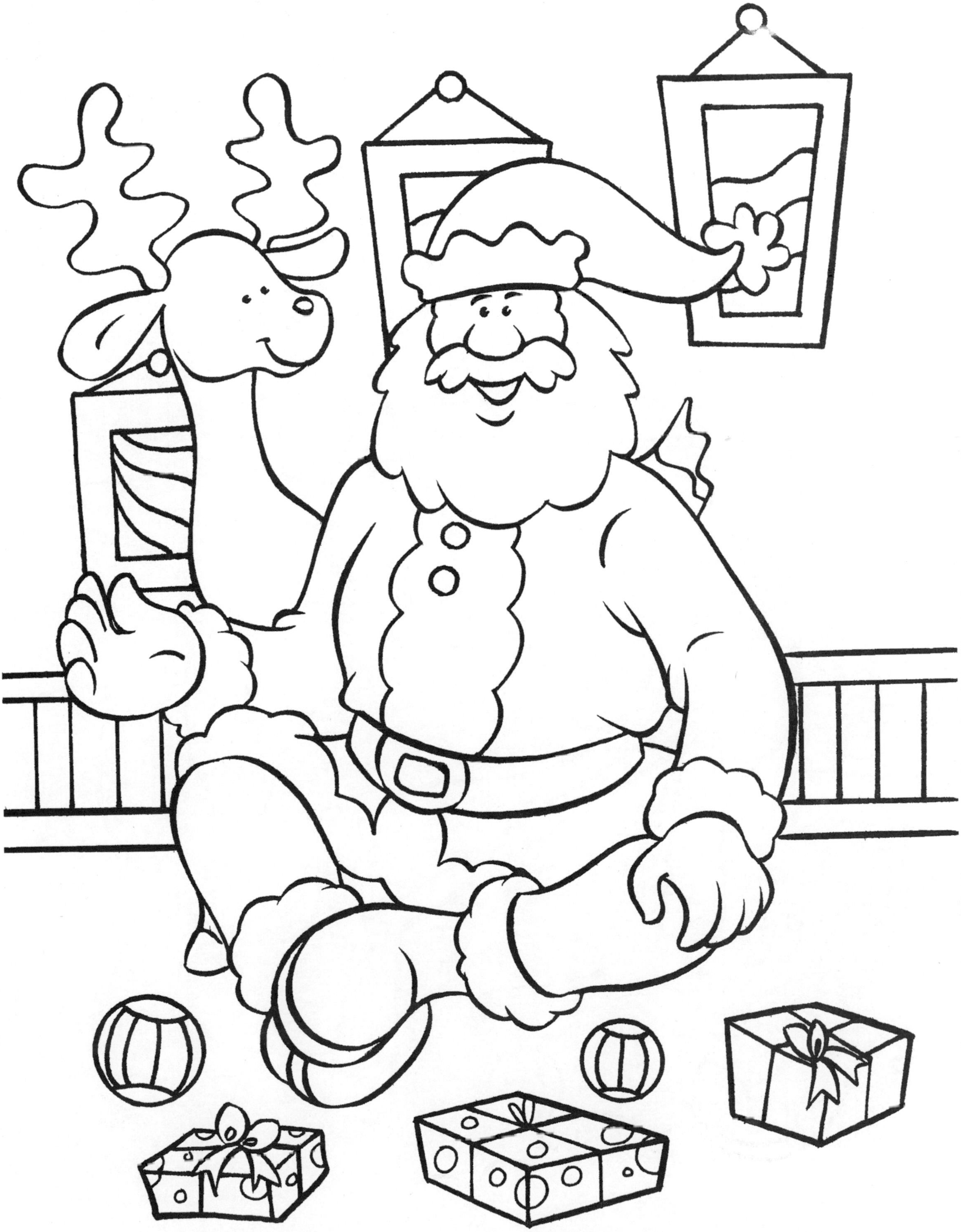

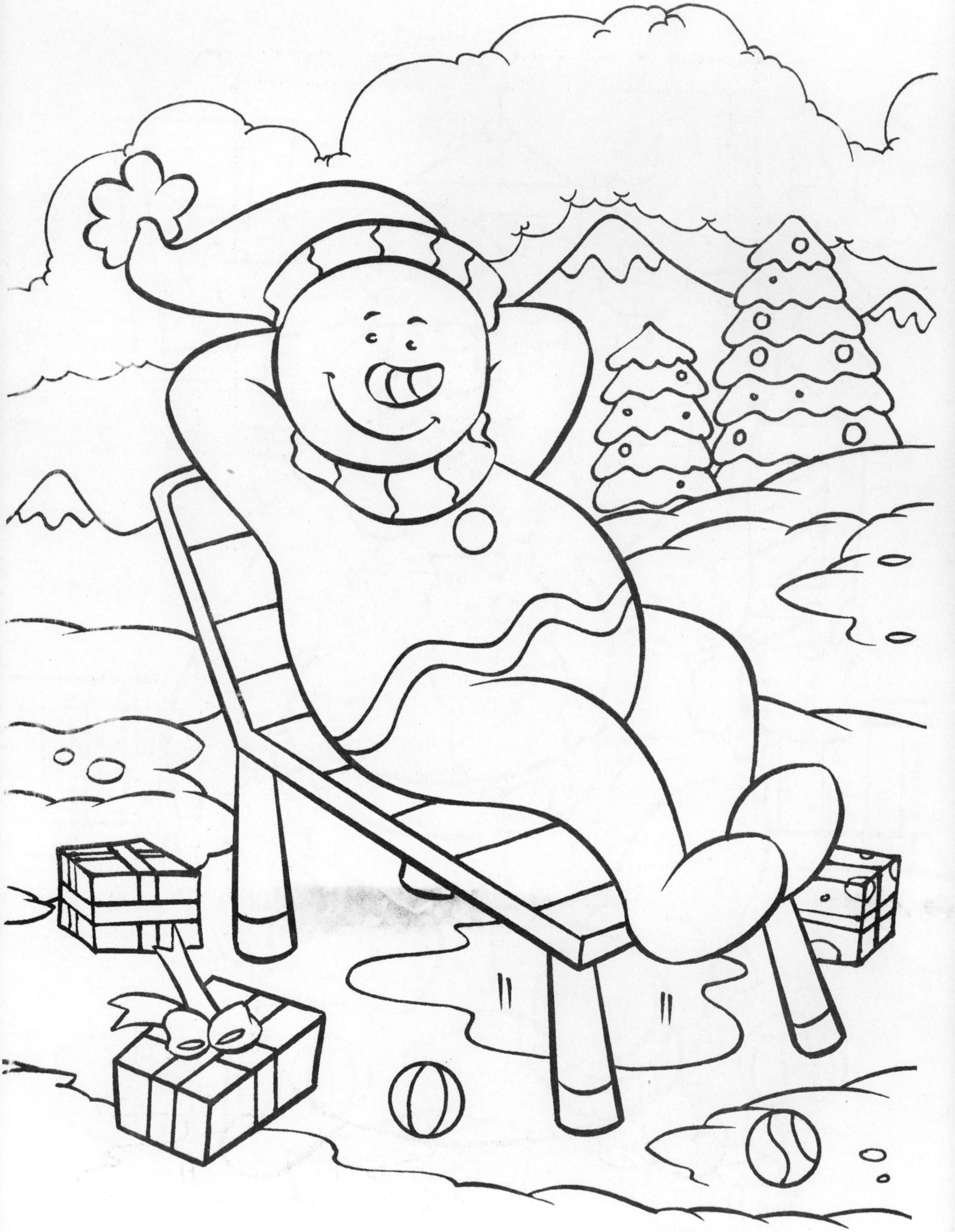

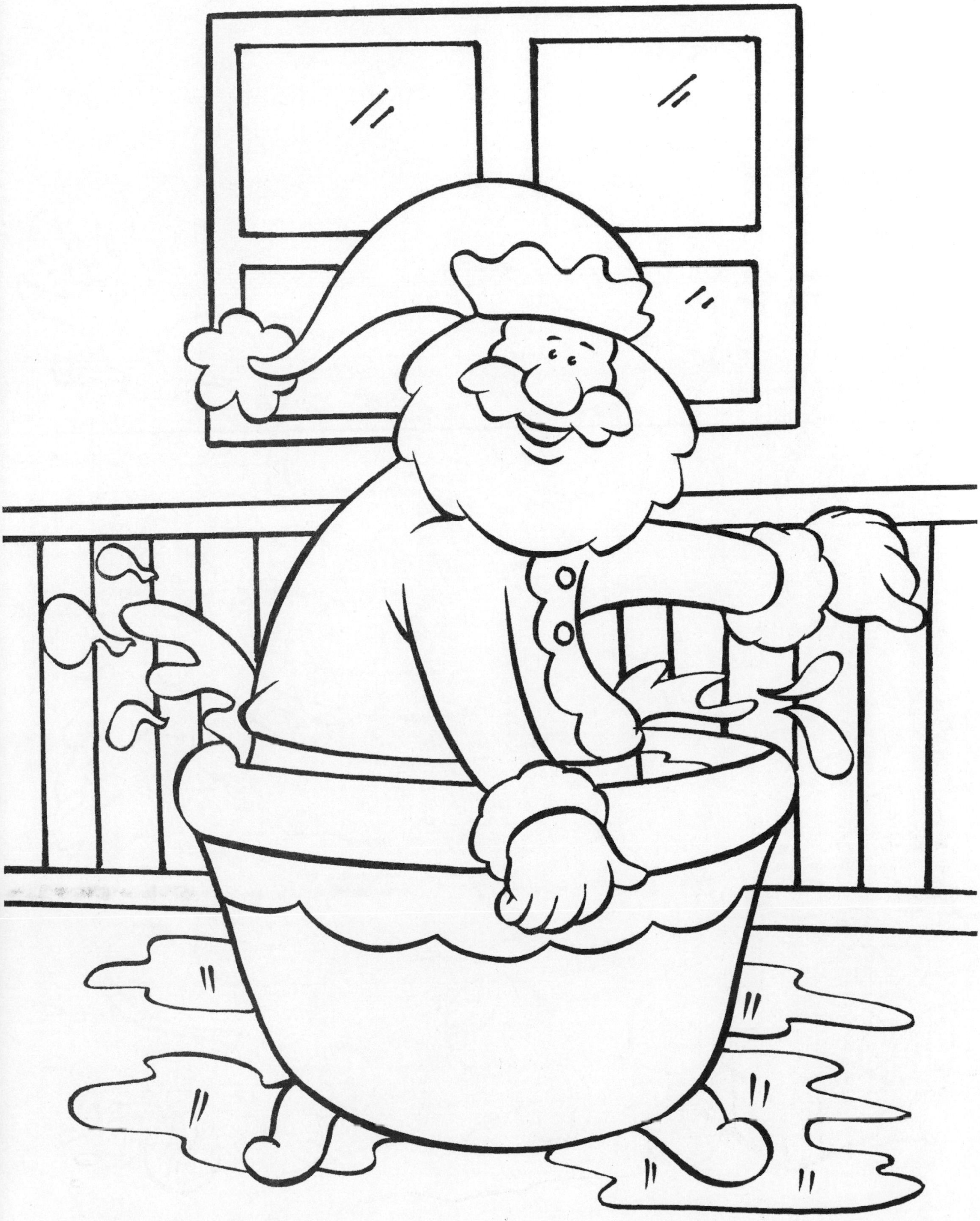

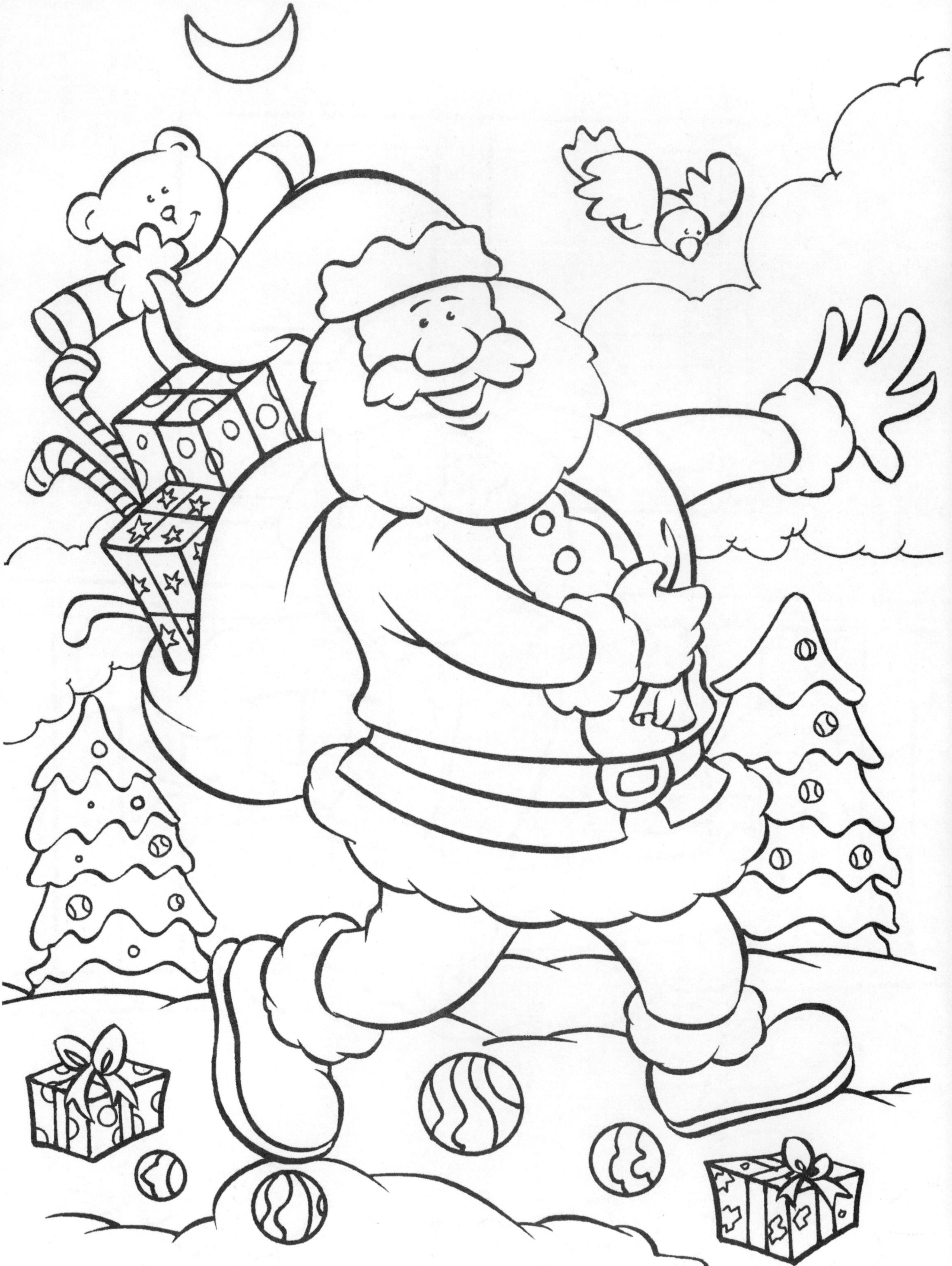

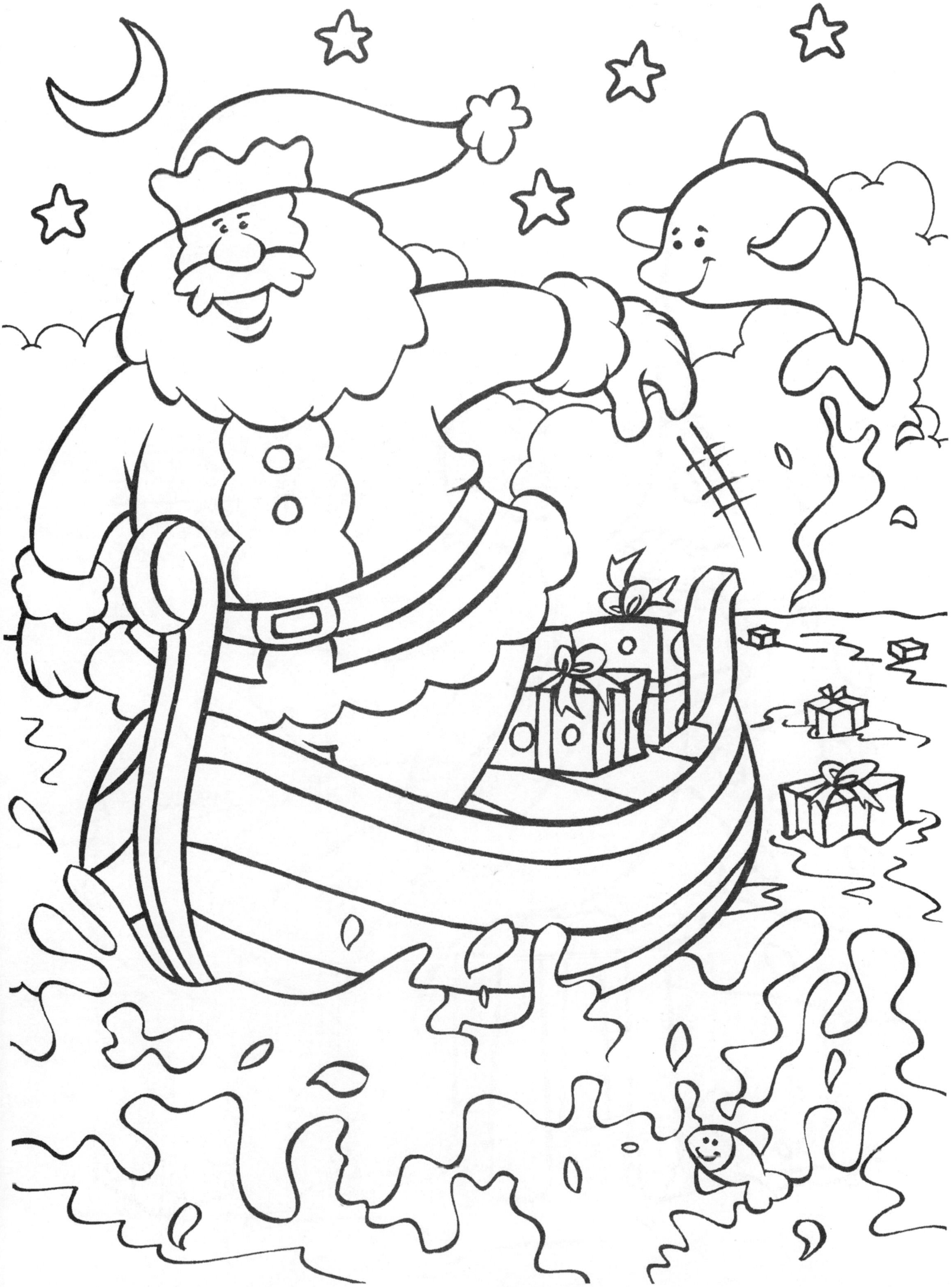

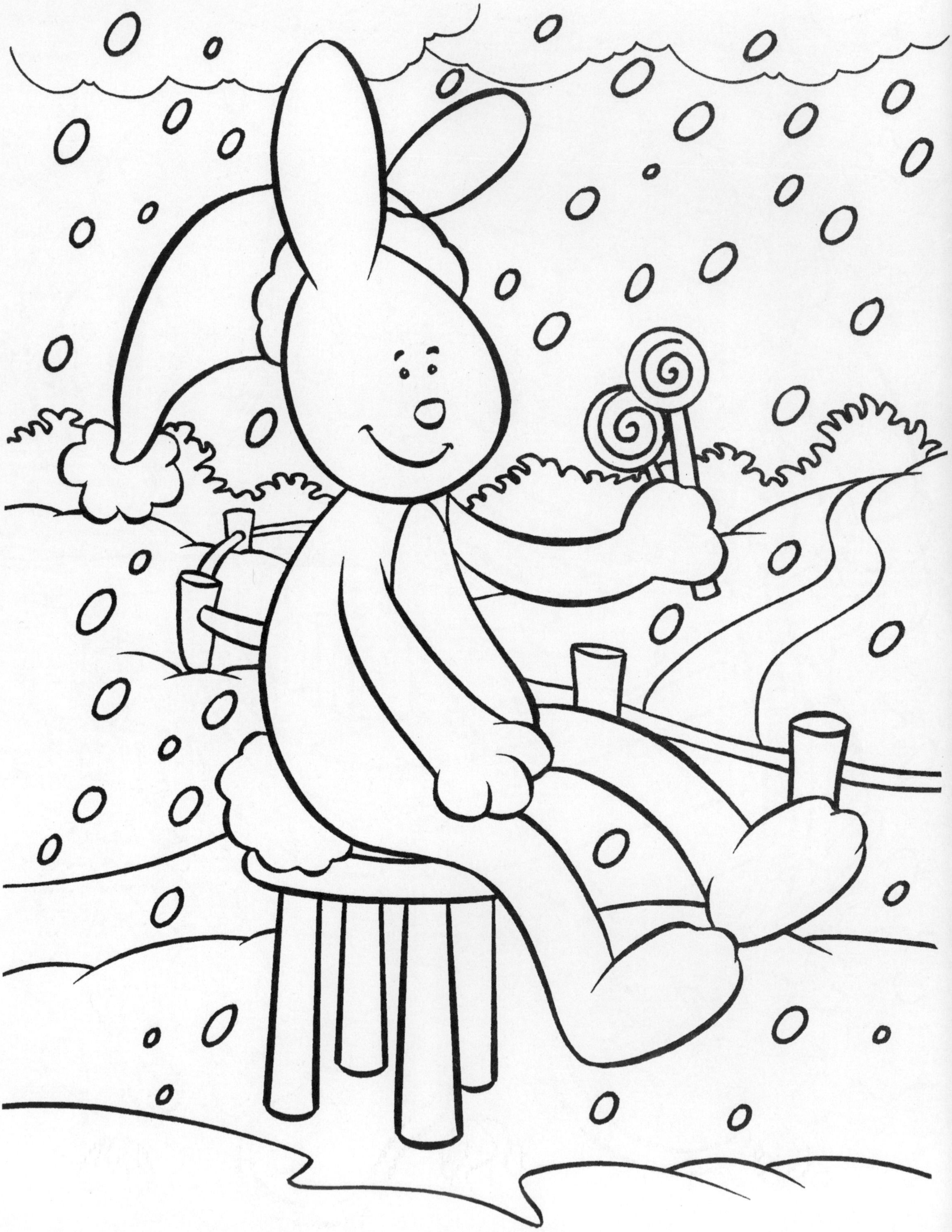

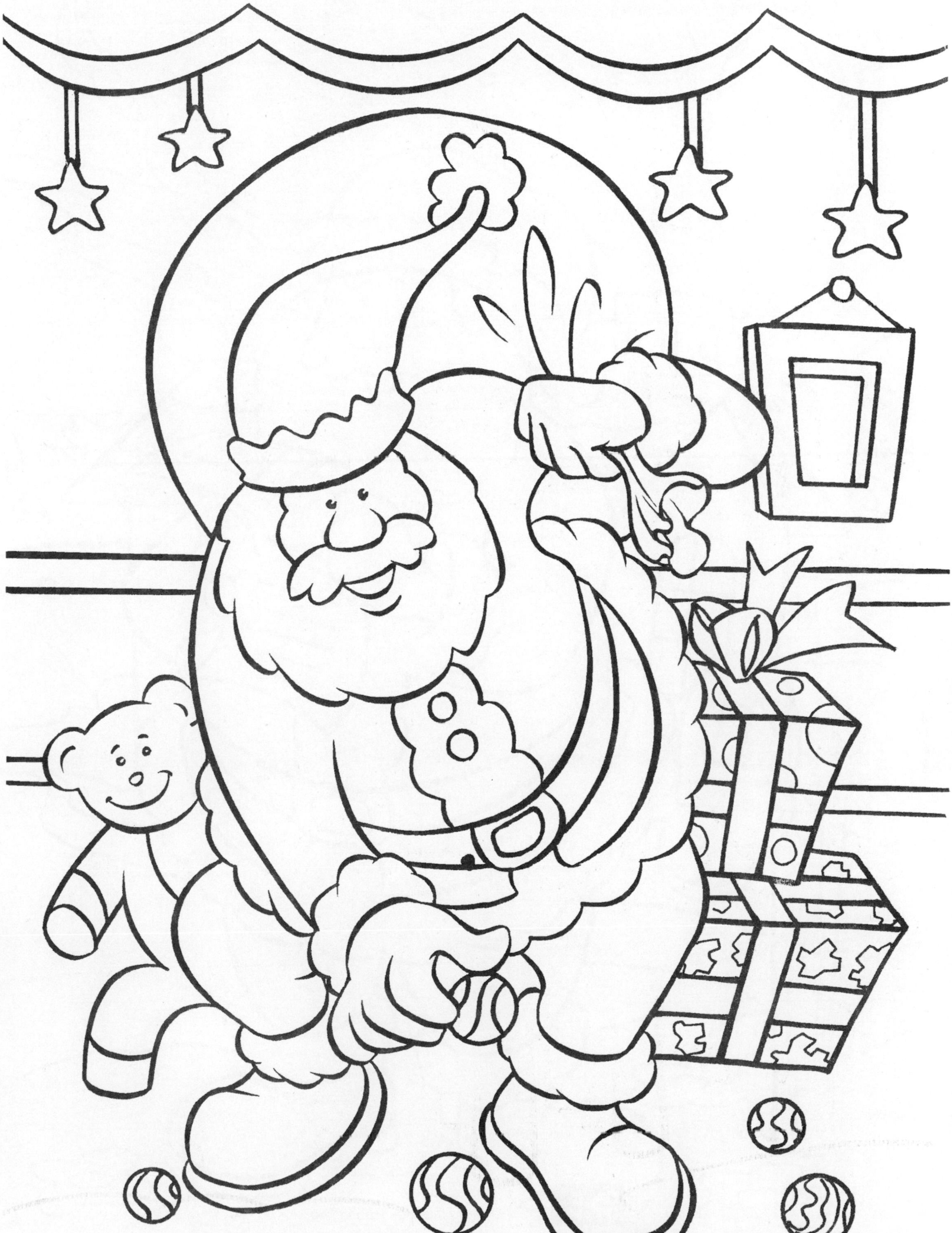

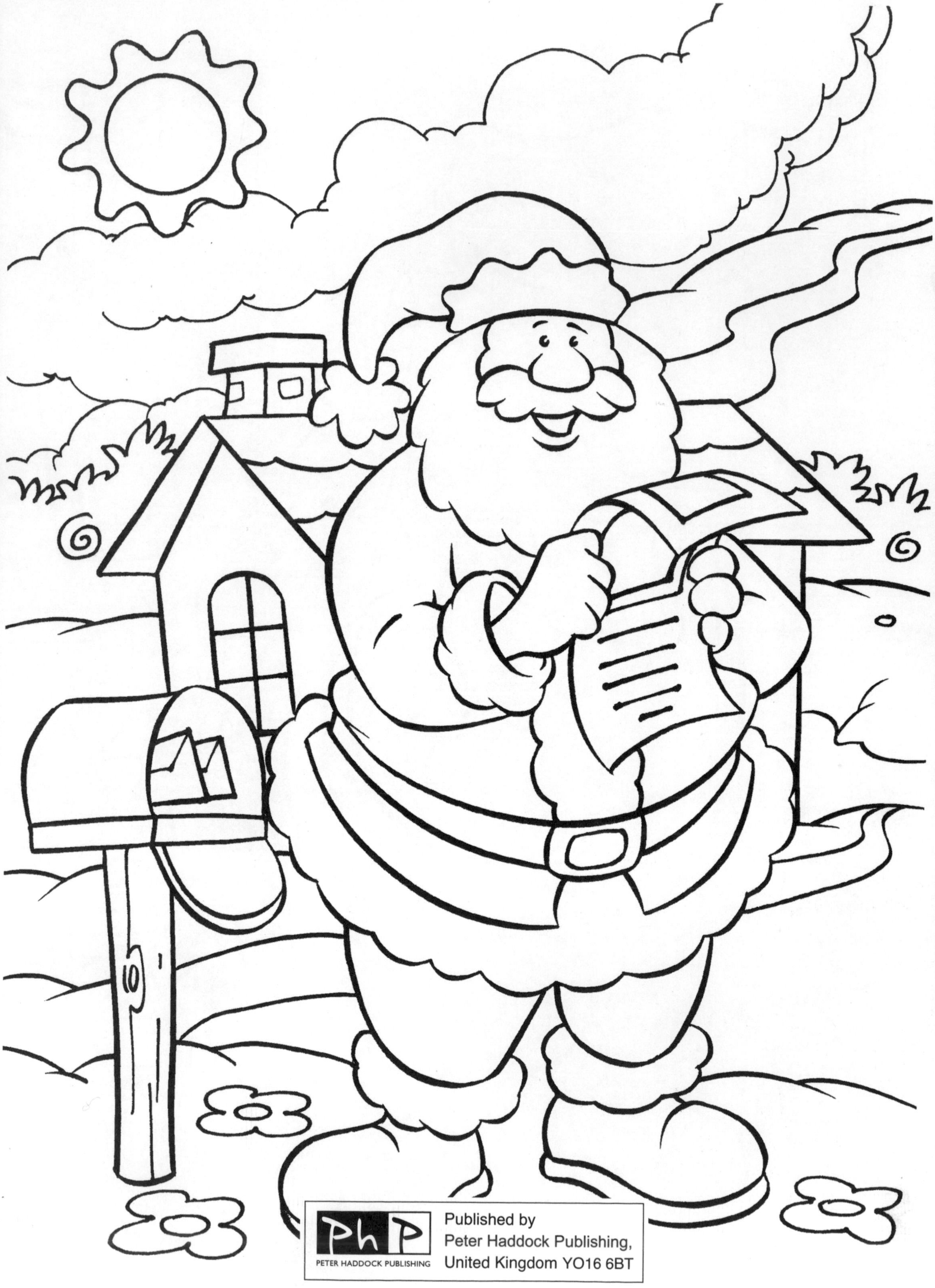

PhP
PETER HADDOCK PUBLISHING
Published by
Peter Haddock Publishing,
United Kingdom YO16 6BT